# Poetry in Motion

Cambridgeshire
Edited by Donna Samworth

Young Writers

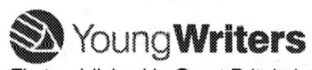

First published in Great Britain in 2004 by:
Young Writers
Remus House
Coltsfoot Drive
Peterborough
PE2 9JX
Telephone: 01733 890066
Website: www.youngwriters.co.uk

All Rights Reserved

© Copyright Contributors 2003

SB ISBN 1 84460 350 4

Foreword

This year, the Young Writers' 'Poetry In Motion' competition proudly presents a showcase of the best poetic talent selected from over 40,000 up-and-coming writers nation-wide.

Young Writers was established in 1991 to promote the reading and writing of poetry within schools and to the youth of today. Our books nurture and inspire confidence in the ability of young writers and provide a snapshot of poems written in schools and at home by budding poets of the future.

The thought effort, imagination and hard work put into each poem impressed us all and the task of selecting poems was a difficult but nevertheless enjoyable experience.

We hope you are as pleased as we are with the final selection and that you and your family continue to be entertained with *Poetry In Motion Cambridgeshire* for many years to come.

Contents

Ailwyn School
Harvey Green (12)	1
Melissa Carberry Dawson (14)	2
Francesca Mann (13)	2
Daniel Conant (12)	3
James Hinton (13)	3
Simon Philpot (13)	4
Cheryl McGee (12)	4
Edward Trafford (12)	5
Adam Conant (12)	6
Kathryn Woodgate (13)	7
Steph Jezewski (11)	7
Roxy Day (12)	8
Chris Meacock (12)	8
Amy Ruddlesden (12)	9
Shaun Wilson (13)	9
Dawn Fisher (11)	10
Martin Aitchison (11)	10
Bobby Tribe (13)	11
Hannah Bruce (11)	11
Natalie Wood (13)	12
Eleanor Powles (11)	12
Laura Rudd (12)	13
Adam Bond (12)	13
Jennifer Ansell (12)	14
Jade Tynan (13)	15
Sam Overall	16
Matthew George (11)	16
Sophie Smith (13)	17
Elizabeth Latham (11)	18
Abbie Harrison (12)	18
Nicola Perry (12)	19
Tom Burrows (12)	20
Tom O'Shea (12)	20
Emma Pollard (12)	21
Hannah Palmer (12)	21
Stefanie Hone (12)	22
Sarah Bloomfield (12)	22
Michelle Bone (12)	23

Amy Broadbent (13)	23
Adam Smith (11)	24
Charlotte Phoenix (14)	24
Jonathan Beardsley (13)	25
Lucie Chapman (13)	26
Steven East (12)	27
Emma Nuttall (11)	27
Hannah Moulds (13)	28
Adam Isaaks (12)	28
James Boon (13)	29
Katie Sawyer (13)	29
Laura Black (12)	30
Niheall Moulding (12)	30
Nathan Wilkinson (13)	31
Daniel Jones (12)	31
Jenna Dockerill (12)	32
Elliott Hicks (12)	32˙
Philippa Murfitt (12)	33
Katy Branch (12)	33
Jasmine Day (12)	34
Tamzyn Christmas (12)	34
Luke Porter (12)	35
Craig Bowd (12)	35
Becca Skinner (14)	36
Ashley Noakes (13)	37
Judith Abblitt (13)	38
Holly Edlin (14)	39
Phoebe Augstein (13)	40
David Ballinger (13)	40
Ellis Lambert (12)	41
Louise Fussell (12)	41
Sydney Moss (12)	42
Gemma Pollock (12)	43
Alice Manwaring (13)	44
Nicholas Vallance (13)	44
Bronte Hellmers (12)	45
Alex Boyce (13)	45
Alex Brookmyre (11)	46
Emily Deboo (13)	46

Chesterton Community College
Nerissa Taysom (15) — 47

Cottenham Village College
Robyn Law (14) — 48
Farrah Sassani (14) — 48
Leanne Evans (14) — 49
Ben Smith (12) — 49
Robyn Afford (14) — 50
Isobelle Anderson (14) — 51
Rachel Wilson (14) — 52
Mathew Dowling (16) — 53
Kayleigh McGinty (12) — 54
Luke Chapman (12) — 54
Josh Blunt (12) — 55
Lorna Thomsen (12) — 55
Louise Thomas (12) — 56
Callum Fisher (12) — 57
Sam Parker (12) — 58
Helena Did-dell (12) — 58
Ed Dimambro (12) — 59
Jacqueline Mason (12) — 60
Peter Willey (12) — 60
Rebecca Hawkes (12) — 61
Matt McCreith (12) — 61
Stefan Wolf (12) — 62
Lauren Ryles (12) — 62
Tom Moller (12) — 63

Cromwell Community College
Sarah Cozens (15) — 63
Thomas Collett (11) — 64
Sophie Morton (11) — 64
Phoebe Ladds (12) — 65
Sophie Butler-Honeybun (11) — 65
Charlie Dawson (11) — 66
Kayleigh Peacock (11) — 66
Aimee Judge (11) — 67
Harriet Muller (11) — 67
Sheree Markham (11) — 68

Amie-Louise Bidwell (12)	69
Morgan Skipper (11)	69
Peter Loizou (13)	70
Donna Venni (12)	70
Victoria Bailey (12)	71
Nicola McDermott (11)	71
Martin Lawrence (12)	72
Jasetta Hood (12)	72
Carl Turpie (12)	73
Hannah Christmas (12)	73
Bianca Parmenter (13)	74
Sarah McAdie (12)	74
Sarah Snow (13)	75
Joanna Turton (12)	75
Francesca Millard (12)	76
Jacob Cavilla (12)	76
Matthew Barnes (12)	77
Kelly Stephens (12)	78
Nikaela Walton (13)	78
Holly Gladwin (13)	79
Daniel Upton (12)	80
Michele Smalley (13)	81
Ben Robinson (12)	81
Natalie Rayner (13)	82
Joanne Pryke (13)	83
Briony Payne (13)	84
Kyrstie Watkins (14)	84
Sandra Lacey (13)	84
Daniel Reeve (13)	85
Joshua Grant (12)	85
Carly Harrison (13)	85
Josie Paynter (13)	86
Chris Chambers (13)	86
Kirsty Earl (13)	86

Netherhall School

Nicola Compton (13)	87
Rachel Kurdynowska (13)	87
Philippa Joslin (13)	88
Ashley Meadows (13)	89
Mark Yao (13)	90

Jasmine Wingfield (12) 91
Mark Streather (13) 92
Lilith Cooper (12) 93

St Mary's School, Cambridge
Eloise Jenkins (11) 93
Sheri Brown (14) 94

Sawston Village College
Matthew Ellis (11) 95
Shaun Poulter (12) 95
Sophie Graham (13) 96
Stacey Attwood (12) 96
Jessica Woodward (12) 97
Russell Boatman (12) 97
Kerry Sayer (12) 98
Jessica Ashby (12) 99
Victoria Brown (15) 100
Joshua Ansell (11) 101
Nicholas Willoughby (12) 102
Ross MacIntyre (11) 102
Alex Stratton (12) 103
David Cousins 103
Paul Munden (11) 104
Catherine McMullan (11) 104
Martin Rolph (12) 105
Charlotte Downing (12) 105
Scott Lansdale (11) 106
Pamela Akita 107
Annie Whyte (11) 107
Jade Field (12) 108
Kate Turner (11) 108
Alice Tasker (12) 109
Rowan Austin (11) 109
Josh Pateman (12) 110
Luke Tancock (12) 110
Claire Green (12) 111
Nicola Slater (12) 111
Lucy Goodchild (13) 112
Katie Sinclair (12) 112
David Phillips (13) 113

Melanie Carder (12)	113
Stacey Kemp (12)	114
Daniel Case (12)	114
Kyle Grainger (12)	114
Shannesse Lane (12)	115
Zoey Demartino (12)	115
Nathan Whitaker (12)	115
Lucas Reali (12)	116
Joseph Ash (12)	116
Megan Ayres (11)	117
Gemma Peck (12)	117
Claudia Cope (12)	118
Liam Flynn (13)	118
Luca Bogen (11)	119
Alex Cracknell (13)	119
Amy Parker (11)	120
Laura Muncey (12)	120
Rachael Colbert (11)	121
Olivia Haddow (12)	121
Josh Bennett (13)	122
Richard Simpson (13)	122
Charlotte Arnold (11)	123
Amy Wright (12)	123
Tom Hawkins (11)	123
Tom Evans (11)	124
Ross Dunsmore (11)	125
Cameron Carr (12)	126
Emma Jacobs (11)	127
Elease Turner (12)	127
Julia Hiom (12)	128
Adam Rice (11)	128
Juliette Colaco (11)	129
Helen Moss (11)	129
Kelly Lloyd (11)	130
Ewan James Baldwin (11)	130
Samantha Tovey (11)	131
James Postle (11)	131
Julia Sansom (11)	132
Karina Honey (12)	132
Freya Chaplin (14)	133
Alexander Scally (11)	133
Emma Clare Pritchard (11)	134

Jazmine Lightning (11)	135
Ellie Seymour (11)	135
George Newnham (11)	136
Hannah Badcock (11)	136
Zoe Wallis (11)	137
Julia Harvey (11)	137
Naomi Chamberlain (11)	138
Charlotte Robinson (11)	139
Patricia Rooker (11)	140
Andrew Cheung (11)	140
Paul Golding (11)	141
Holly Martin (12)	141
Kayleigh Owen (12)	142
Cody Gibson (12)	142
Ryan Stubbings (12)	143
Gemma Hollidge (12)	143
Stuart Chamley (12)	144
Rebecca Thompson (12)	144
Boin Lee (11)	145
Mechelle Earl-Human (12)	145
Hanna Taylor (13)	146
James Shelford (11)	146
Matthew Wilkinson (13)	147
Emily Simmons (11)	147
Adrien Webster (12)	148
Natasha DeMartino (14)	149
Daniel Shaw (12)	150
Victoria Paulding (13)	151
Maheen Sattar (13)	152
Lee Evenden (13)	152
Chloe Pantazi (13)	153
Lee Graves (13)	153
Samuel Jeffrey (13)	154
Matt Smith (13)	154
Jonny Munden (13)	155
Daniel Chatten (11)	155
Umit Koseoglu (13)	156
Sarah McCrae (13)	156
Charley Collier (13)	157
Rosie Ball (13)	157
Daisy Ives (13)	158
Katie Cheung (13)	159

Abigail Hunt (13)	160
Callum Rookes (12)	160
Lucie d'Heudieres (13)	161
Jessica Smith-Lamkin (13)	161
Matt Teversham (11)	162
Victoria Toombs (12)	163
Maria Reali (13)	164
Josh Warner (12)	164
Tanya Browne (12)	165
Viktor Simonic (12)	166
Cameron Ford (13)	166
Lara Nugent (12)	167
Yousif Oghanna (12)	167
Samantha Coupland (12)	168
Nadiim Varsally (12)	168
Kerry Chapman (15)	169
Susannah Worster (11)	170
Molly Wright (11)	171
Kerry Bond (11)	171
Kayleigh Sawkins (12)	172
Emily Reed (12)	172
Rachel Chaplin (11)	173
Thomas Andrew (11)	173
Hannah Griggs (15)	174
Bai-Ou He (14)	174
Gemma Pluck (12)	175
Nicky Savill (12)	175
Alistair White (14)	176

Soham Village College
Rebecca Blyth (14)	177
Philippa Hunter (13)	178
Alex Belshaw (13)	179
Hannah Rowley (13)	180
Danielle Theobald (13)	180
Hannah Sewell (14)	181
Kelly Bridge (14)	181
Richard Clarke (13)	182
Sophie Brown (12)	183
Lewis Cotterill (13)	184
Amanda King (12)	184

Sarah Claydon (14) 185
Amy Ellis (14) 186
Ben Reed (12) 187
Arianne Martin (12) 188
Adele Doughty (12) 188
Daniel Bocking (14) 189
Richard Leadon (12) 189
Thomas Winter (12) 190
Mary Ross (12) 190
Bradley Anderson (13) 191
Jamie Ingram (12) 191
Christopher Gannon (13) 192
Beccy Dobson (13) 193
Matthew Taylor (13) 194

Swavesey Village College
Jess Piggott (12) 195
Sobia Artrey (13) 196
Olivia Jones (12) 197

The Perse School For Boys
Peter Alston (13) 198
Tom Wilshere (11) 199
Sam Baron (15) 200

The Perse School For Girls
Beatrice Bottomley (11) 201
Helen Maimaris (12) 202
Claire Cocks (11) 202
Harriet Lavis (12) 203
Abigail Stacey 203
Zosia Krasodomska-Jones (12) 204
Victoria Noble (12) 205

The Poems

Suicide Letter

Well that was it, that was my life
And I ended it after twelve years,
I left that woeful world behind.

I believed it, and so I relieved myself of such a
                                  prosecuting painful life
And when the time came near to taking my life
I bottled it, who wouldn't, but then stood up to
                                  those powerful bullies,
By taking the cowards way out.

But at least they will feel as bad as, as bad can get since,
It was they, their fault, now they can carry this terrible
                                  tide upon their shoulders.

Let them grieve like I once grieved, let them have that
                                  stainful pain,
They will be powerless and in great vain they will
                                  share there pain upon my grave.
Knowing all along that my life would not be long.

Well that was it, my life of pain, where bullies reigned
                                  and had great fun,
While others wandered off into the shadows and never returned.

So I ask you this,
Why are there bullies? What makes one person better than the other?
Nothing, some would say and they are right but in the modern world,
It's everything, money, strength, popularity, good looks, all of these
And many more.
But people say nowadays, that they have some of these, but
In the modern world today if you don't have everything,
                                  you have nothing.

Harvey Green (12)
Ailwyn School

The Lion In The Sea

Happiness is the lion in the sea,
It is shining blue and with a white crusty mane,
It makes a joyful noise as it hit
The gentle rocks upon the sandy shore.
The sky is getting dark,
The sea begins to calm
As the peace curses the sandy shore.
The lion is sleeping, sleeping in the peace and quiet,
The lion wakes
He is in despair,
He is annoyed,
He has disturbed the curses
Of silence on the sandy shore.
He lashed at the rocks
With the speed of lightning,
When the children came,
He is at peace once again,
He was at peace once more.

Melissa Carberry Dawson (14)
Ailwyn School

The Elephant

He tramples along the dusty track,
Dust and mud crackles on his back,
He is as old as a crumbling shack.

The trees are watching like owls at night,
He runs right out of all their sight,
They all look up to his great height.

Francesca Mann (13)
Ailwyn School

The People's Voice

That dreadfully happy warning sound,
Again,
Warning of pain and heartache to come,
The night sky lit up by searchlights,
Searching for hope of an aeroplane,
That in all its glory goes,
Into that night sky laden with bombs
And releases its hell into the depths of cities,
Showing innocent people inviewable images,
No, this is not a war where we are all courageous,
Or where we all fight with honour,
We need not suffer,
Just because some supposedly sane lunatic
Thinks he himself owns the world,
This is the voice of the people,
The voice of the nation,
The voice of the world.

Daniel Conant (12)
Ailwyn School

Peace

Peace is a snowy owl
White fluffy with big green eyes
Sitting in the snow on a mountain
Quietly looking out alone.

Peace is a snowy owl
Waiting for prey to arrive
It is very quiet as still as a rock
Until its prey arrives.

James Hinton (13)
Ailwyn School

When I Was Young

When I was young and cheerful,
I liked the grass green hills,
I would run up the hill and roll back down,
For hours and hours I played on the hill,
Until my mum would say, 'It's time to go now,'
I would wave goodbye to the animals,
Smell the country air and then I would depart.

I am older now and when I return to the hills,
I am not ablaze, 'Wow it's a hill,
My mum has dozed off under a tree,
The animals are concealed in the forest,
Instead of rolling down the hills,
I walk around lifeless with nothing to do,
Later on my mum awakes
And it is I who wants to go.

Simon Philpot (13)
Ailwyn School

The Fairy Garden

How soft the moon shines down on me,
How beautiful the night!
How wonderful the garden looks,
When bathed in silvery light,
How stunningly the fairies dance,
All in a circle round,
How mystical the garden looks,
When the moon shines down
And when the fairies drift away
And day has just begun,
How dazzling the garden looks,
When basking in the sun.

Cheryl McGee (12)
Ailwyn School

Living In A Disposable World

That can's empty,
Now let's throw it away.

That balloon's burst,
Now let's throw it away.

That packet's empty,
Now let's throw it away.

That pen's run out,
Now let's throw it away.

That paper's torn,
Now let's throw it away.

That bike's got a puncture,
Now let's throw it away.

That computer's old,
Now let's throw it away.

That car's old,
Now let's throw it away.

This planet's been stripped of its resources,
Now let's throw it away!

Edward Trafford (12)
Ailwyn School

Life

A cloudy view,
A happy sad time.

The joyful glee
Of succeeding,
The lovely sensation
Of winning,
The terrible time
Of bereavement,
The distraught feeling
Of failure.

The pitter-patter of rain,
The pleasure of scrumptious sunshine,
The horrendous hail and
The soft, slushy snow.

The youngness of a toddler,
The naïveté of a six-year-old,
The stropiness of a teenager,
The strength of an adult.

Life goes on,
Or so they say,
They lie
It stops.

Adam Conant (12)
Ailwyn School

A Sonnet About David

My sweet and loveable friend called David,
You are the sweetest apple of my eye,
In me, you bring out the innocent kid,
Your cool brilliance that we cannot buy,
You make me feel like a bird that can fly,
This sad and lonely sonnet is for you,
I would do anything, I would die,
My love for you is brilliantly true,
Our great bond together no one can break,
I even need you more than a best friend,
The golden walls of big Zeus we could mend,
When I fall down and hurt you help me mend,
For dear David I would give my whole life,
Some summer day I wish to be your wife.

Kathryn Woodgate (13)
Ailwyn School

The Morning

I see a misty street,
Hills are rolling away,
On my left all I see,
More and more houses.
On the field is an early party,
Adults moving to an outside disco,
Always on the street is rubbish,
Left from someone's party.

The wind is cold,
As the leaves rustle,
The rich green hills far away,
I love those hills,
I want to live there,
That is where, not here, there.

Steph Jezewski (11)
Ailwyn School

The Old Pool

We drove into the car park
And I saw a large building,
My family all walked in
And the lovely clean smell of the pool
Drifted over to us,
Ten minutes later I was in the pool,
Playing with a football,
The sounds of laughter echoed around the room,
Whilst I was splashing around being
Taught how to swim.

The pool's not the same any more,
It's small, expensive, my family is not there,
The floats, the balls and all of the laughter
All seem to have drowned.

Roxy Day (12)
Ailwyn School

The Pier

I went to the pier with my dad today,
The smell of the sea and sound of the waves,
Sizzled my senses like sausages in a pan
Enthralled by fishermen with their rods on the rail
And McDonald's afterwards for tea.

I went to the pier with my dad today,
But it's not what it used to be.
The fishermen no longer thrill me
And the waves are second best
And no more McDonald's for tea.

Chris Meacock (12)
Ailwyn School

Painting Bedrooms

Today I started to paint my room,
I used to love doing this,
Picking up the roller, slapping it into the
Wonderful bright blue paint,
I thought it was great, rolling it onto the bare walls,
Smelling the strange scented paint.

Now I paint the walls and know not to apply so much paint,
Gently dip it in and paint it up, down, up, down,
It doesn't smell different and exciting anymore,
That strange varnish smell has drifted away
It's just a colour, not bright and bold, just another job to do.
The novelty has worn off but my newly decorated room is beautiful.

Amy Ruddlesden (12)
Ailwyn School

Winter

The snow is white, there's cold in the night
As children dream on icicle swings.

A lonely fox dreams, asleep on the snow-lit grass,
In the city stars creep through the darkness.
Through the night the snow looks like glass
As frost overtakes the buildings and cars
And the night is ridden with stars.

Christmas Day comes and goes,
The road is still covered with snow.

The fox has gone and so has the frost and snow,
The starlit night grows shorter
And leaves on the trees appear round the English border.

Shaun Wilson (13)
Ailwyn School

My Great Grandma

I can see a clear blue sky with a glittering
Sun shining in my eyes,,
On my left is a photo of my great grandma
Who I never got to meet.
I feel different, like someone is watching me up above,
Sometimes I feel that my great grandma
Is there watching me,
It is 1.30pm in the afternoon,
I can see far, far in the distance,
In the sky, a face that looks like my grandma,
With a kind face,
I feel like my grandma is watching me from
Up above, trying to guide me,
Like she's trying to tell me something.

Dawn Fisher (11)
Ailwyn School

Goodbye

I walk around the empty bedroom
Look out of the window and what I see,
Is an old brown shed
And an old apple tree.

It's weird seeing the space
Where my bed used to lie
But not anymore
And I start to cry.

A voice calls out
'We can't wait anymore'
And for the last time,
I close my bedroom door.

Martin Aitchison (11)
Ailwyn School

The Beast

In a village to the east,
Was visited upon by a vicious beast.
His eyes reflected the light
And a glance and smell of death,
Of a chosen one.

Flames licked up round the church spire
And the congregation's line of defence
Was overcome by fire
There calmly stood the priest by the fire
He died for his god

There was a crimson light surrounding the
Huge paw and the evil best crept
Slowly towards the wooden church door.

Bobby Tribe (13)
Ailwyn School

Cold

It is raining really hard,
I see animals running away,
I want it to stop raining,
I hear the rain hitting the floor,
I am in the pack,
In the distance I see houses,
I don't like it when it's raining,
I feel cold,
It's really dark,
I am on my own,
I know it's early in the morning,
I see a lorry,
Where am I?

Hannah Bruce (11)
Ailwyn School

Reflective Poem

There I see her
Staring back at me
I don't know who or what she is
All I know is that she is like me.

Every move I make
Every step I take she does it too
She stares back at me
She is looking very sad
And starts to cry.

I sit down, she stays standing up,
I start to talk to her,
'Are you alright?' I get no answer
We sit there for hours.

I can't think of anything to say
I walk off leaving her
She calls my name
I still ignore her.

Natalie Wood (13)
Ailwyn School

School Days!

First lesson tired and lazy,
Then after that it's just a bore,
Break time all pupils are crazy,
Then third they're sent out the door,
Lunch break there's a rush of people
Running through the hall,
Next you get teachers telling you
About your uniforms,
Last lesson, pile up the homework,
Then out of school you go,
Waiting for another school day
And going to bed as told.

Eleanor Powles (11)
Ailwyn School

My Best Friend

My best friend means so much to me,
She is always there when I am sad,
When I need help we will talk over tea,
Quite often though she can make me mad,
She's my best friend and will always be there,
Through good times and bad, we'll help each other,
We will have quiet chats because we both care
We share secrets we don't share with our mothers,
No matter what, you will always be there,
We're in a good crowd and share a good laugh
Loyal we are, that makes us a pair,
We laugh at most people, even the staff,
We will definitely be friends forever,
Our friendship will last, and hateful never.

Laura Rudd (12)
Ailwyn School

Kipper The Cat

Kipper is my cat, he is very fine,
His fur is grey, his paws are white, just right,
The neighbours feed him but I know he's mine,
Sometimes when I call him, he's out of sight.

Kipper is very lively for his age,
Kipper is the boss of all cats here,
When I do homework, he sits on the page,
When Kipper is near, the cats are in fear.

He rolls around in the dirt when it's hot,
He shelters from the rain when it is wet,
Kipper lies in waiting for a bird to spot,
His tail sticks up on end when he's first met.

One eye is very dull, the other bright,
I think he is nice to look at first sight.

Adam Bond (12)
Ailwyn School

Life Is A Roller Coaster Ride

At the first age your ride has just begun,
Life doesn't seem that much fun,
As a babe you're being gently rocked,
Just like the ride crawling out of its locks.

A child looks up for parental support,
'Mum, what does this mean? Dad had I ought?'
We're off to school, we're on our way,
It's all uphill, learning each day.

Your heart starts pounding as you approach the peak,
Just like a teenager in love, feeling weak,
Parties to go to but nothing to wear
And what on earth shall I do with my hair?

Schooling is over, it's time to have fun,
Twisting and turning on the downhill run,
Chatting and joking and dancing in clubs,
Talking and dating and drinking in pubs,
But the ride suddenly drops from the height of your life,
Give up being best now and look for a wife.

The fifth age is the most hectic of the group,
There's twists and turns and loop-the-loops,
With mouths to feed and work to be done
And just enough time to have some fun.

When your kids have grown up and they all have left home,
The sixth age begins, you're on your own,
The ride is bumpy and going downhill,
Have you noticed, you're always ill?

The last of your ride is coming quite near,
You can't really see, you can't really hear,
The train and the carriage go back into the locks,
Your roller coaster ride finally stops.

Jennifer Ansell (12)
Ailwyn School

Who Am I?

I have been through misery,
I have been through pain,
I don't need no one messing my life up again.

So I don't need you
To help me fall
All I need is someone to see me through.

No one listens
No one cares
You think I am not good enough
But I know I am worth more.

I need a real friend
Who will listen to my problems
But it's hard to find that person I am looking for.

So I hope you understand
That I don't want you in my life
So now I won't let you make me cry no more.

I have listened to your tears
Helped you through your pain
Now it's time to finally be myself again.

Jade Tynan (13)
Ailwyn School

The Greatest Hamster

I love my hamster, she is so cute,
Maggie's teeth are sharp as carving knives,
Her fur is long and grey is her suit,
She's as fast as bees coming out of their hives
And she nibbles at her cage every night
And spins her wheel until the morning,
She sees in the dark with her great eyesight,
She goes to the toilet without warning,
Her feet are so small they slip on the bars
And her whiskers are so long and have a small curl,
When I first got her, she had a small scar,
Her big black eyes make you want to spin and whirl,
All these things make her the best hamster ever
And of course she has brains, which makes her clever.

Sam Overall
Ailwyn School

What's Going On?

I can see a moonlit street,
On my left there is a dark and misty alley
Branching off the pavement,
There is no sound, there is always sound.
What is going on?
It is a typical night with a full moon high in the sky,
I can see a figure moving slowly towards me in the mist,
What's going on?
I feel scared and lonely,
The same thought whizzing through my mind,
What's going on?

Matthew George (11)
Ailwyn School

Crushed

Cry in a corner,
Lonely and scared,
Tears rolling down,
In a cascade of fear.
Soul torn to shreds
In a matter of words,
Caused by the ignorance
That others possess.
Marooned on an island,
Of malevolent hatred,
No lifelines to pull you from
Their whirlpool of despise and loathing.

Share your problems with another,
Trust in their authority,
To sort out the dilemma you are facing,
Don't bottle your pain
In a package of poison,
So you will never again exist,
In a dimension of invisible darkness and ice,
Fill your world with rich sunshine,
And live your happy life in
Peace!

Sophie Smith (13)
Ailwyn School

Who Or What?

I see nothing but darkness
And a shadowy white figure to the left of me,
But then a burst of red light almost blinding me,
Sometimes it moves, sometimes it is still,
I just turn cold, freezing cold,
What should I do, no one is awake?
The figure seems to be coming towards me
It has a beard, hawk-like eyes and straggly hair,
I feel alone, scared,
I wish this creature would go leave me be,
Poof - the creature was no longer there,
I still dream of a white figure on that path,
Even now the same chill goes down my spine,
The one that went down my spine when I was a child.

Elizabeth Latham (11)
Ailwyn School

Where I Want To Be

Where the sea meets the sky
Where the seagulls fly so high
Where the beach looks so nice
Where it looks like paradise.

I gaze upon the world with my eyes
I smell the air which smells like spice
I hear the whispers, they are so wise
I feel free, I realise.

This is where I want to be
This is what I want to see
This is why I've got to be me.

Abbie Harrison (12)
Ailwyn School

Light Up The Sky

It's time to light up the sky,
They explode and then they die,
Colours bright, colours strong,
Light up the sky all night long.

Noisy bangs, oohhs . . . and aahs . . .
Shooting high, like sparkling stars,
Crackling sticks and spinning wheels,
Exploding rockets add to the thrills.

Bonfires built to last the night,
Oozing lots of warmth and light,
Standing in the cold night air,
Wrapped up warm they come to stare.

Baked potatoes, soup to sip,
Hats and gloves prevent the nip,
Children's smiles stretch ear to ear,
They've had to wait a very long year.

Red, gold, silver and green,
Colours the brightest you've ever seen,
Sparkling, shimmering, shining too . . .
Fireworks for me and you.

Nicola Perry (12)
Ailwyn School

My Cat

So cute is my cat who I love so much,
Who lays on my bed all day and all night,
He's furry and warm and soft to the touch,
His eyes are dark green and shine in the light,
He goes by the name of Tibby Tyler,
He's moody and sulks when Daisy is here,
He hisses and spits and spikes up his fur,
He loves his warm milk but runs from sweet beer,
He's got a girlfriend with eyes bright green,
She comes in our house and eats all his food,
When they're together others are so mean,
They're all so jealous and get in big moods,
My cat is so cool and also the best,
Because he's mine, he's better than the rest.

Tom Burrows (12)
Ailwyn School

My Family

In my house there's my two sisters and me
Jessica and Amy are their two names
They fill up the house with laughter and glee
Messing around and playing silly games.
We live in Ramsey town, down in Field Road
We haven't lived there long, only two years.
In our garden there is a big fat toad
It jumps out and brings my sisters to tears.
We have barbecues and family parties:
Hot dogs and burgers, eating lots of food.
For desserts the girls like to eat Smarties
And if not they will get in a bad mood.
Although sometimes we can be quite snappy,
As a family we are very happy.

Tom O'Shea (12)
Ailwyn School

Poem

Shakespeare was the greatest,
Will was the best,
I think that this poor old man,
Deserves a great *big* rest!

Most people think he's boring,
Obviously not me,
I can't understand how,
People would rather watch TV.

Romeo and Juliet,
Where for art thou?
Come on, quickly!
Hamlet, take your bow.

In Will's stories,
Things are not as they seem,
This is what he pointed out,
In a 'Midsummer's Night's Dream'.

Emma Pollard (12)
Ailwyn School

Flowers

Blowing in the wind whilst bowing their heads
Beautiful colours dancing in the sun
Bright red roses standing in their beds
People come and enjoy the sun with fun.
Lovely tulips magically growing
Red, blue, yellow and purple, all shining,
From your window you can see them glowing,
Also you see their beautiful lining.
Blowing in the wind, splashing in the rain
Shining in the sun and still looking fine.
Driving down the road through the leafy lanes,
Hope dreams come true by making wishes mine,
Still up on the hilltops standing so proud,
The heads of sunflowers looking at clouds.

Hannah Palmer (12)
Ailwyn School

The One

You are the person I can talk to,
You are the person who listens to me,
You are the person who helps me get through,
You are the person I wish to be,
When I drift off to sleep, I dream of you,
They are exciting and wonderful,
You always say to me what we can do,
Draw me a picture, nice and colourful,
You are the one, you are the one I desire,
Why can't you be mine forever and beyond?
You make me feel like I am on fire,
If you can't or don't be mine, I won't be fond,
Say you'll be mine or I will be so sad,
If you don't love me then I will go mad.

Stefanie Hone (12)
Ailwyn School

Minty

I know that you don't speak but you can hear,
I wish that you could always be around,
The love that we share will always be near,
What would I do if you hadn't been found,
I will always and forever love you,
I will love you for as long as I live,
I hope that you will always love me too,
I'll always be there for you and to give,
I am scared that I might not find you there,
Before within your eye, I've seen a tear,
I'll always be there to share and to care,
Don't be scared Minty, don't have any fear,
I know you have some annoying habits,
You will always be my favourite rabbit.

Sarah Bloomfield (12)
Ailwyn School

Life

Life is precious people say,
Treasure it in every way,
People come and people go,
In three years or maybe tomorrow,
No one knows what life will bring,
This, that and anything.

Life is precious people say,
Treasure it in every way,
Things can go wrong,
For short times or long,
Things can go right,
Without a fight.

Life is precious people say,
Treasure it in every way
Because anything and
Everything is life!

Michelle Bone (12)
Ailwyn School

Stick Insects

Thin and fragile like a lollipop stick,
So many species, take your pick.

Camouflaged like a swaying ghost,
Some are found near the coast.

In many colours, green and brown,
And yet, they are just a simple noun.

Eating bramble in the trees,
Moving peacefully in the breeze.

Clutching cautiously side to side,
Some do fly, and some do glide!

Amy Broadbent (13)
Ailwyn School

Britannia

Mud covers the fields that were once golden,
The treasures of conquerors now all but stolen,
Ruined are dwellings that were once grand,
As great armies of men sweep over the land.

Scarlet pools stain the stones,
For the ground is littered with their bones,
The iron fist of men of power,
Now unclenched for the warrior's devour.

Where great houses were, there is but rubble,
Where brave men stood there is but graves,
Where giants of the empire ruled so strong,
Now all of them are dead and gone.

The smouldering villages cease to burn
And the stench of death is all but gone,
The warriors have taken what was left behind,
Of the greatest civilisation of their time.

Adam Smith (11)
Ailwyn School

The Leopard

She stalks her prey with
Outstretched arms,
Walking near the tall, green palms,
While her baby cubs she gently calms.

Her cubs follow her with pride
And never leave her gleaming side,
A love that for all time will abide.

Charlotte Phoenix (14)
Ailwyn School

The Ghost Ship

As night fell
The ghost ship sailed across the moonlit sky,
Carving a shadow,
A shadow of fear across the deserted town,
Turning the moon into a lethal silver blade
Slicing through the clouds
On to the abandoned town below.

The sails ragged
Shreds of cloth stained with red blood,
The mast, eerily tall,
Glistening in the moonlight.
The captain standing at the bow of the Golden Ram,
Laughing evilly at the sight of people
Cowering with fear miles away.

The ship's crew
Standing behind the captain,
Their cutlasses dull in the moonlight,
Red with blood
And the skull and crossbones
Waving boldly in the night air.
The last anyone saw of the ghost ship,
Was when it faded in the misty
Grey horizon.

Jonathan Beardsley (13)
Ailwyn School

Home Alone

I'm alone at home,
Feeling pretty sick,
Mum and Dad's at work,
Wish they'd come home quick!

Wouldn't let me go to school,
Thought it would be fun,
Feeling pretty bored now,
Think my faking's done.

Must be nearly teatime,
Can you hear the sound
That my stomach's making?
Food must be found.

Feeling pretty scared now,
Been alone all day,
Can't help hearing noises,
Wish they'd go away.

I'm all alone at home,
Feeling pretty sick,
Mum and Dad's at work,
Wish they'd come home quick!

Lucie Chapman (13)
Ailwyn School

The Snake

Nights are now longer, the summer is done,
The long winter sleep just days to go now,
The season is finished, the battle is won,
Fill up her belly, the way she knows how.

Slithering slowly in the darkest night,
Seeks out the food to take hunger away,
Lights from the highway make others take flight,
If only the mice would come out to play.

A rustling of leaves from a log nearby,
Both silent and deadly she moves ahead,
The twitching of whiskers and glint of eye,
The mouse has no chance, for soon he'll be dead.

Fast as lightning and without further thought,
In the beat of a heart the mouse is caught.

Steven East (12)
Ailwyn School

Farewell To Summer

The blackened clouds are forming,
Soon the rain will fall,
Summer is departing,
But first please hear this call,
I have had a great summer,
Water fights and all,
Sunbathing in the garden,
Swimming in the pool.
Camping out at Tallington,
Windsurfing too,
I have had a great summer,
I hope you did have too!

Emma Nuttall (11)
Ailwyn School

Cat And Mouse

I have a big, silver stripy fat cat
Who chases a furry burgundy mouse
The cat always lays on a yellow mat
And all this happens in a big blue house.
The cat is sure to catch the mouse one day
The mouse has only one safe place to hide
My cat will fetch the mouse, but he will pay
The mouse has his friend, the dog, by his side.
He is very angry at the chasing tom
He stops him hurting his little furry friend
He surprises him, giving him a bomb
The fighting pair drives the mouse round the bend.
An end to the fighting must be found soon
After all it is only a cartoon.

Hannah Moulds (13)
Ailwyn School

Fishing

I go fishing sometimes
And I'm not bad
But we catch a lot of slime
Just me and my dad.

Sometimes we stay long
Because it gets really late
And we can't see if the float is gone
Or if it's just our weights.

And then I wish
While I'm sitting there
That I will catch a big fish
Anytime, anywhere.

And I'll keep wishing,
And I'll keep fishing.

Adam Isaaks (12)
Ailwyn School

My Dog

My dog is white, just like the white of snow
He loves to run and jump around the house
He's got a collar just like a dickie bow
He will hide if he sees a mouse.

His eyes are odd, he looks like a weird dog
His nose is wet and is as black as paint
He is weird and looks like a scary frog
He is so weird he makes me want to faint.

My sis says he's handsome and needs a snog
But I say, 'Why, he's only a dog!'

Despite this I love his shiny fur
Though his eyes are odd, he's thick as a log
Some days he is scared by the cat's purr
But he's cute and I love him, he is my dog.

James Boon (13)
Ailwyn School

Mum

Her arms go round me for protection
She keeps me safe and warm on a cold night
She makes sure I don't get an infection
She makes sure I win every single fight
She is full of wisdom and helps me through
She is beautiful and intelligent
She helps me in the things I want to do
She says nothing that's irrelevant
She makes my bed and irons my clothes
I love her very much, she is the best
When I have got a cold, she wipes my nose
She even passed her second driving test
I think my great mum is a lot of fun
And I think the sun shines out of her . . .

Katie Sawyer (13)
Ailwyn School

My Mother

She is really very nice my mother,
Although she is very small and petite,
Not as large and tall as my brother,
He has enormous size eleven feet.

She does a lot and even cooks and cleans,
Even though she still has a lot of fun,
She sometimes does her work in her old jeans,
She even sometimes goes for a run.

My mum always makes me have a nice day,
Even when something really bad is near,
She makes everything seem nice and OK,
Even when I worry and also fear.

So mother never go away, please stay,
So don't go until the end of your day.

Laura Black (12)
Ailwyn School

Music

Music is nutritious
Music is nice
Music tastes delicious
With that extra spice
Drums in the song
Makes your feet tap
People like to sing along
But it's hard if it's rap
Some people like to sing
Some people like to dance
Music is a beautiful thing
Please give it a chance
The moral of this song, maybe you don't know
If you have no music, then you cannot grow.

Niheall Moulding (12)
Ailwyn School

My Dog Buddy

The greatest friend you could know ever hope to know,
Black and tanned, sharp face and pointed ears.
He walks tall and proud just like he's on show
And prances around like a giant deer.
Small dark eyes that are shiny, bright and alert,
He loves to run, chase and play with a ball,
He likes to play in water and dirt,
That is why I love him, he is so cool,
His long black hair makes him look like a bear,
His long bushy tail is just like a broom,
Loving and friendly, let him show he does care,
Let him into your heart I know there's room,
He looks kinda fierce but don't be afraid,
Once you meet him, you'll be glad you stayed.

Nathan Wilkinson (13)
Ailwyn School

It's All Going Wrong

He kicks the football as hard as he could
It is going in but no it has missed
It flies right past the goal and hits the wood
The crowd start to boo and some even hissed
He drops his head in shame, jogs back with his team
The keeper kicks it out, it heads for him
Oh no this is a nightmare and not a dream
He controls the ball and passes it to Tim
He runs down the line and waits for the ball
The crowd stands up and start to scream and shout
Tim runs right past him and doesn't hear his call
Suddenly Tim stops and starts to look about
Tim passes it to him and he kicks the ball
It has found the net, hooray the crowd call.

Daniel Jones (12)
Ailwyn School

A Sonnet - My Pets

I love my dog, Rosie, she is the best
Taking her for walks is a lot of fun
Before I got her, I never would have guessed,
How exciting it was to see her run.

I love my horse, Biscuit, he is the best,
Walking or trotting we have lots of fun,
Cleaning and grooming and then for a rest,
Spending time together come rain or sun.

I love all my goldfish out in the pond
Thirteen or fourteen, I always lose count
Sitting and watching we always bond
The splashing of water out of the fount.

I love all my pets but which one to choose?
I can't pick one, so no one will lose.

Jenna Dockerill (12)
Ailwyn School

Sonnet

One day I saw her picture in a book
Her face was very hairy, black and brown
I shook and thought that I should have a look
I travelled all the way to her home town.
Her mouth was big, her tail was very long
Her nails were very sharp, her paws were soft
Her breath was smelly, she had a big tongue
Her nose was black, she was smelling a broth.
She always likes to play a game of ball
One of her ears was broken, what a shame,
When she's excited she runs to the hall
It was very hard to pick her a name,
I don't care if she looks like a warthog
She will always be my cuddly dog.

Elliott Hicks (12)
Ailwyn School

My Weekend In The Lakes

This weekend I went a-walking,
Up over the hills and dales,
My sister kept on talking,
As we wandered on up the trails.

When we started it was sunny,
With a view across the lake,
When we got to the top it wasn't funny,
As the rain made soggy our cake.

By the time we started down we were ready,
For relief from our aches and pains,
But we found ourselves far from steady,
As we slipped on wet rocks in the rain.

When we reached the bottom, we fell into the car
And exhausted, looked forward to a drink in the bar.

Philippa Murfitt (12)
Ailwyn School

My Cat

When my cat was ill, she went to the vet
My cat used to sit upon the chair
Then I got a hamster as a new pet
Now we have a tigger upon the chair.

She licked her paw and stroked it
Through her fur
I remember my cat with great fondness
When I went to bed I could hear her purr
And could feel my heart fill with sadness.

As she got old, she needed lots of care
The bear on the chair reminds us of her,
I'd like to remember her, do I dare?
It's not our cat because he has no purr.

Oh how I really miss my tabby cat
And how she used to lay on my black hat.

Katy Branch (12)
Ailwyn School

My Kitten

My kitten has fur so shiny and black,
He runs and bounces all around our house.
Every time I call him he comes back,
He just wishes he could have caught that mouse.

His big round eyes are like saucers so green,
His claws so long and sharp grip anything,
The smallest panther I've ever seen,
He is nice until he scratches my skin.

He eats all his food in five seconds flat,
By the end his nose is covered in cream.
Soon he curls and falls asleep on the mat,
Lies for hours chasing birds in his dream.

His cute little paws have the softest touch,
His name is Chester, I love him so much.

Jasmine Day (12)
Ailwyn School

Boo Boo

Trots along does she, proud as can be
Head up straight, ears down firm, eyes open wide,
Her eyes are like marbles, round and dark,
Dark like mist, like a chocolate button
Body as hazel as caramel
Sparkles in the light, stands out real bright,
Soft, but rich, like a million bucks
Tail out crocked, not curved like a hook
Feathered like a bird, only softer
Feet like goats, light black pad underneath,
Boo Boo her name, comes when I call her
Smile on her face wagging her little tail,
No dog is perfect, only some come close,
In my eyes Boo Boo is as close as they get.

Tamzyn Christmas (12)
Ailwyn School

The Sun

Something so beautiful, something so high,
Something so delicate keeps us alive.
He watches us from his house in the sky,
He is our guardian, he helps us survive,
Orange, red and yellow what about blue?
Swirling and twirling high up in space,
Do not forget that it's destructive too
And it is loved by the whole human race,
Beautiful outside and ugly within,
Probably made by angels with love,
Two parts of passion and one part sin,
Living peacefully floating above,
But as he grows old it soon comes to die,
Nobody cries not even a sigh.

Luke Porter (12)
Ailwyn School

The Countryside

A tractor is ploughing in a field,
Getting ready for the seeds to sow.
The farmer hopes this year for a good yield
And the rain and sun so that the seeds will grow.
In a nearby paddock a pony stands eating hay,
His coat all glossy and black in the light,
Then munching on grass for the rest of the day,
A warm, cosy stable awaits him that night.
Birds fly swiftly across the sky,
With a gentle breeze beneath their wings,
Where do they go to? I wonder why.
The countryside is full of amazing things,
Just open space as far as the eye can see,
This is the perfect place where I want to be.

Craig Bowd (12)
Ailwyn School

Darkness Rages In Me

The night is dark,
It is dark and dull,
No signs of life,
The dead trees wave,
A hard, cold breeze,
Makes everything screech.

I stare at my father,
Stuck in the ground,
The dead, still flowers,
Wilting around,
His gravestone grey,
Hard to read,
His joy once lived,
Where is he now?
I cannot be sure.

He was not a thief,
Nor angel, nor devil,
Just an ordinary man
Who did nothing wrong.

My heart is pounding,
No love,
Bleeding,
The warm days have gone,
They went weeks ago,
It has been night for me.

My father was my all,
My home,
My idol,
My father.

It came as a shock,
I keep reminding myself
Was it my fault?
Where was mother at a time like this?
She had left years ago,
Shortly before the days had gone,
Father and I loved her,
Dearly,
He could not cope,
And now he's gone.

Becca Skinner (14)
Ailwyn School

Loveless World

The lonely sky of hopefulness
The stars are laughing at joyfulness,
Whoever stays in my land, I will forgive anyone.

The only way of full love,
Is to find a dark cove,
Nowhere to go, but here.
The crashing waves of darkness,
Plummeting the world of nightmares,
Into an everlasting world.

Warfare, joyfulness and victory,
Are all the pleasures you can't enjoy
Nothing can separate the world to a
Loveless world.

Ashley Noakes (13)
Ailwyn School

The Gift Of Peace

War is destruction, selfishness and hurt bundled together,
War is anger and want tied in a knot,
War is heartless misery destroying so many,
War is unjust.

Loneliness is emptiness and sadness all in one,
Loneliness is no one to help you when in need,
Loneliness is the lack of comfort or reassurance,
Loneliness is emptiness.

Need is the necessity of something that has to be delivered,
Need is reaching for something you cannot do without,
Need is the aching heart, desperate to be cared for,
Need hurts.

Friendship is helping the needy, loving the unloved,
Friendship is healing the sick by the warmth of your heart,
Friendship is giving without receiving,
Friendship is effortless joy.

Happiness is knowing joy and delight stitched together,
Happiness is trusting and innocent,
Happiness is peace and kindness,
Happiness is love.

Love is the feeling of tenderness given freely,
Love is gentle, kind and sharing,
Love is relief to pain inside the heart,
Love is for everyone.

Peace is happiness, wrapped in a parcel, tied with a ribbon,
Peace is the feeling of friendship and love inside your heart,
Peace is knowing that someone will be there for you in the
Time of trouble,
Peace is a gift.

Judith Abblitt (13)
Ailwyn School

Tremble

I *see you,*
Lying motionless,
Stiff and *cold,*
I'm sorry Trems.

It is hard to believe that
You were once *happy,*
Hopping
Warm and *joyful*
Bringing tears,
Different to the ones I shed now.
I'm sorry Trems.

                Your ears - once floppy,
                        Ears.
                How I loved your ears.
              They aren't floppy anymore.
                  I'm sorry Trems.

                                I could have saved you
                                But I'll always *remember*
                      Your fluffy little face, nudging into mine
                            The way you ran after us,
                                  Played games with us,
                                      Honking *happily.*

                But now you're gone
                    I'm sorry Trems.
                      I love you.
                  My tremble bunny.

Holly Edlin (14)
Ailwyn School

The Unknown Fear

It starts with butterflies in my stomach
And a flinching in my heart.

Like someone's walked over my grave

And then it begins
The grass is *long* and *thick,*

I am running
And shrinking.

I have *cold* feet and a colder heart

I feel worry, doubt, suspicion and dread
I panic, and try to run faster.
                    But I'm getting s-l-o-w-e-r!
It is an appalling, excruciating feeling.

My heart will take no more
And then, my eyelids flutter and my heart begins to slow
I stir and am aroused from my nightmare once more
I return to reality.

Phoebe Augstein (13)
Ailwyn School

Cuckoo - Haiku

Cuckoo callously
Calls, cuckooing crazily,
Consistent cuckoos.

David Ballinger (13)
Ailwyn School

NOS-Fest

A quarter mile of jet-black tarmac
Could be an urban road or country lane,
Both sides packed with the young and daring,
Blondes and bleached blondes, along with tattooed boys,
And at one end stand the men and their toys.

The chequered flag goes down, tyres scream,
Foot down hard, gear stick clenched,
Nos button on and the speedo hits the ton,
Flames burst out into the warm summer night.

The finish line in sight,
He's lived his dream,
The Mitsubishi in his mirror,
It's the end of the high-octane fight.

Ellis Lambert (12)
Ailwyn School

Autumn

The morning air was sweet against the chilling wind
The deep yellow sun, peeking over the horizon,
As the birds sang their songs while perched on greenless branches,
The few remaining leaves took their last breath
And fell into the sea of brown, red, yellow and orange,
The few patches of grass left were cold and soaked in morning dew,
The families awoke, children, parents, babies,
The children were in the garden, playing in mounds
Of dead leaves, with red noses, hats and scarves,
As the day went by, the day grew cold and dark . . .
And once again, a leaf fell to the ground . . .

Louise Fussell (12)
Ailwyn School

Waiting Kitten

Small bundle of fur
Waiting at side of the road.

Cold and alone
Crying and wet.

Dying of hunger and thirst
Scared.

Homeless
Scared of the cars rushing past,
Scared that she may not find a home
There she
Waits in the patch of brambles
A sneeze and a cough
Waiting,
Waiting,
Waiting.

Waiting for the car to stop
And take her home
Waiting for the warm milk and tuna
Waiting for the chair by the fire
Waiting for someone to love.

Sydney Moss (12)
Ailwyn School

Shadows

I hate to see the shadows at night-time
They scare me half to death
All those different shapes and sizes
Moving in my room.

The other night my cat walked in
Making a big scary shadow
It arched its back
And made a monster.

Then my dog walked in
Moving slowly
Staring straight at me
Making a dragon.

Then all of a sudden
Something big walked in
I knew it was going to hurt me
It made a 'woo' noise.

The big shadow was getting bigger
It was getting closer
I flicked the light switch
It wasn't a shadow it was my big sister Amy.

Amy was just trying to scare me
It worked though
She got into a lot of trouble
So I put a spider in her bed.

Gemma Pollock (12)
Ailwyn School

Why?

Why is the Earth round
And not flat? Why am I a
Girl and not a
 Boy? Why
 Am I hungry
 And not
 Fed? Why
 Does the colour
 Of my skin
 matter? Why
 don't I
 Know the
 Answers
 To these
 Questions?

Alice Manwaring (13)
Ailwyn School

Football

He
darted across the field as the
referee blew his whistle. Spurred on by his red and
white fans screaming at him with their painted faces. He broke
through their defence with a swift dodge that cut them in two. He
was triumphant, he would score, he would be the crowd's hero, then
with a sickening crunch, he went tumbling down as the force of the
blow made him scream with agony as he rolled across the muddy
surface. There was a sharp pain that swelled up his body into a
spark of anger ignited into a deep fire which exploded in
him. Causing him to launch a punch, the red card was
shown and he walked with the crowd booing
him.

Nicholas Vallance (13)
Ailwyn School

Friends

Friends . . .
    Friends . . .
        Friends . . .
Keep them close to your heart . . .
    The more friends you have the
friendlier you are . . .
    You look after them
        They look after you
They are like stars . . .
    They are always there for you . . .
        They help you when you need them to . . .
    Friends . . .
    Friends . . .
    Friends . . .
        I love you all . . .

Bronte Hellmers (12)
Ailwyn School

Sunken

Skipping home on a summer's day
I got closer to the darkness
It was definitely doomsday,
I figured out the shapes hiding in
The black shadow.
I didn't need to hear it,
I'd seen it in their blurred sorrowful pits,
But in muffled whispers they told me.
My heart sank, taking me with it,
The pool was soon filled,
Quickly it overflowed
I would move on and fill another,
Then the voice of doom appeared,
It screamed the wretched word over and over
It spun in my head.

Alex Boyce (13)
Ailwyn School

Football Forever

Football is life,
Life is football,
Nothing can pull us apart,
Come rain or snow,
Win or lose,
Avoid the dreaded draw.

On to the field,
It's three o'clock,
On a Saturday afternoon,
A darting run,
A screaming goal,
Hear the home crowd roar.

The season ends,
Top of the league,
Cups and medals galore,
Top scorer, me,
Best in class,
That made the others sore.

Alex Brookmyre (11)
Ailwyn School

Silent Friendship

The noise of silence;
Makes a buzzzzzzzzz
When you're alone.
Friendship, taken
And, all that is left
    is
        you . . . alone.

Emily Deboo (13)
Ailwyn School

The Black Hawk Watches

As the black hawk watches
She glides the water
Only blue silk separates
The icicles of her fingertips
A crown of thorns on her head
A drop of blood slides down her black cheek.

The black raven calls her name
As he soars above the black wood
Beneath her feet along the path where she walks
Logs of brittle wood, sodden with the storm
That brews in the sky
Eaten alive by beetles in the black ground.

She whispers songs to herself
In whirlpools above her head
She hears his breath upon her shoulder
Quiet and still, these ancient walls.

She turns to fade him and they run
The bramble cutting the flesh of her ankle
She runs with her black prince through the black wood under the sky
As the black hawk watches.

Nerissa Taysom (15)
Chesterton Community College

Tracing Rivers

Little fingers, tracing rivers,
Into China, out of China.

High in an aeroplane, looking down,
Bigger fingers, tracing old rivers,
Flying into China.

Orange deserts and purple grapevines.
Towering red rocks and lush green valleys.
Mountains and rivers,
Where blue sky meets grey wall.

High in an aeroplane, looking down,
Bigger fingers, tracing old rivers,
Flying out of China.

Back to the billiard table, back to Cambridge,
To read stories, and watch travel programmes
And dream and dream of

Little fingers, tracing rivers,
Into China, out of China.

Robyn Law (14)
Cottenham Village College

Morocco

The blazing sun glistens on the sand of the Sahara,
Tourists pile into the packed market squares of Casa Blanca,
Spending their money like there's no tomorrow,
She wears a black headscarf, her heading burning in the dryness
And a few miles away, a world full of tourists,
Know nothing about the real me
And my people who slave away for the tourists
Like Egyptians building a pyramid
A pyramid that will never end,
I am Morocco.

Farrah Sassani (14)
Cottenham Village College

Walking In Morocco

Walking over the burnt, dried land
Mountains towering high in a hazy mist
A river flowing through an arid land
A green lush oasis in strips surrounded by the brown
Barren earth.

Walking into a small village
Greeted by warm, dark, friendly, smiley faces
The smells of spices, the sound of music,
Like the sound of the storm.

Fruits grown in an explosion of colour like a fireworks
Display
The smells hitting you with a shock like jumping in a
Cold pool.

Mint tea made by women you'll never meet
Looking through a glassless window
Watching people travelling on mules on winding roads
Reminding you of a time you never knew.

Leanne Evans (14)
Cottenham Village College

The Mission

Go ship, go to the unknown foggy darkness
Go and cut through the darkness.
Take and carry the stars with you
Do not turn back from the face of death.
On no account lose this battle
Refuse to back away
Fly into the starry night that goes on forever and ever.
Protest against the cold-blooded evil out there.
Let the light from goodness shine down
And clear the evil from people's minds.

Ben Smith (12)
Cottenham Village College

The Flowing River

I am the sunshine,
Glistening over the desert,
I am the feast,
A large, fat pheasant.

I am the paved, narrow street,
The carefree attitude of the place,
The Mafia man,
With his staring face.

I am the ocean,
Lapping the beach,
Crawling and creeping,
But still can't quite reach.

Walking back and forth,
Shoes tied around my neck,
Along the beach,
Watching the sunset.

Warm air touches my skin,
Spices touch my nose,
I look at large mosaics
And still the river flows.

Robyn Afford (14)
Cottenham Village College

The Islanders Of Sicily

Floating gently onto the beach
Down the sand coated narrow steps,
Mingling with the rippling dunes.

The shoes tied around my neck,
Laces tied together,
Feet sliding through the sea like small hands squelching butter.

Inside the vast, cavernous cathedral - spiralling to new heights,
Draped in small glass mosaics, biblical mosaics, dominating mosaics
Soaring to new heights.

Amongst the tranquil shell of the island, work must go on and on.
Old, weary men follow glistening snail tracks
Through the deserted streets of the white washed towns
Till that snail is on a table at a restaurant
And the men replay the endless hide-and-seek.

Roman columns line the edge of sparkling cliffs,
Water creating a disco of colour against its walls.
Arabs, Moroccans, Norman's moulded together to create the ruins,
Ancient temples, pale against the limitless blue of the sea.

A visual feast washed down with a string of Sicilian delights,
Baked aubergines as soft as the sand,
Prickly pear as sharp as the eyes of the village children

Sicily.

Isobelle Anderson (14)
Cottenham Village College

The Colours Of China

In a valley, lies a tunnel of vines,
Arches of grapes - deep purple in colour,
Sweet to taste and the aroma of wines.
But far away, where eyes cannot see,
A world of contrast is out there.
There's a desert with shimmering heat
Making the sand ripple and move,
And huge red rocks and golden sand please the eye.
But far away, where eyes cannot see,
Lovely blue lakes, blue pine trees tall
And mountains rising above them all.
Locals wear blue outfits and caps
And take photographs of everything.
But far away, where eyes cannot see,
Old ancient cities and destroyed ruins.
Beautiful Buddhist caves with Buddha painted on the walls
But far away, where eyes cannot see,
Different cultures meet - nature and civilisation meet.
Every fabulous holiday has to end
And the adventure is over.
But still the memories will stay forever.
Now, it seems we'll have to go home,
Back to the atlas to trace the rivers
Across a country of colours.
Because far away, where eyes cannot see,
A world of contrast is out there.

Rachel Wilson (14)
Cottenham Village College

The Life Within A Page

That can't be so! A life with a page
A single page that explains everything you've done
No, never! Life is only existent with age
No one could comprehend what you've become
Or could they?

The key to success is never through that door
The feeling of regularity slowly hits home
The constant pressure and demanding for more
The horrible shiver, of feeling alone
The feeling of want and improvement
The better use of the world perfection
The money income to pay the rent
The loss of faith and misdirection

The feeling to love and lose
The moments of greatness ebb away
The decisions in life that we must choose
The feeling of wanting awakes a new day
The knowing of what's to come
The understanding of why things are
The success for the things you've done
The looking up and wishing upon a star

Life cannot be written on a page
Life isn't as consistent as this poem
The time will soon come for change
I just hope I will be there to see it
For this is my life, my page.

Mathew Dowling (16)
Cottenham Village College

Go Song, Go

Go song, go song, to the very tip top!
Go; knock people off their feet
Go; be danced forever by children,
Take with you the groove of the night,
Do not be quiet, be loud and stick in people's mind,
On no account stop people dancing for their lives,
Refuse to stop make people's nights,
Dance like an angel in Heaven,
Do not let the TV beat you,
Protest against old music reaching people's ears,
Give love to people who are sad and lonely,
Create music like we've never heard before,
Yes, go song, be wild and free
Celebrate your freedom and creativity
And above all remember to make people want to dance and sing.

Kayleigh McGinty (12)
Cottenham Village College

Spaceship

Go ship, go to the planets, no one has ever been to before.
Go to the planet's core.
Carry with you the hopes and dreams of the team back
                                        at space control.
Do not go near to the black hole.
On no account must you come back until your job is done.
If you refuse to do this, you will be lost in space.
Whizz in and out of planets like a bee through flowers in a garden.
Create the space station, make it the best.
Yes, go back to the Earth.
Celebrate the mission that has been completed safely
And above all remember to be careful.

Luke Chapman (12)
Cottenham Village College

Go Ship, Go . . .

Go ship, go to the unearthly perimeter of space.
Go and explore the darkness of the unknown.
Carry with you the souls and aspirations of the fearless navigators.
Do not hesitate in the face of danger.
On no account turn back to the anticipating spectators
Awaiting the return of the vessel back on planet Earth.
Refuse to believe the tales and stories
Which experienced pilots tell of their horrifying periods
In this mystifying atmosphere.
Speed like a wild stallion into the depths of the untamed blackness.
Protest against all hardships and fear
Which meet you on your journey of toil and strife.
Make the world a more knowledgeable place
By researching and experimenting with these extreme conditions.
Celebrate these fearless young men!

Josh Blunt (12)
Cottenham Village College

The New World

Go book, go to a reader who'll read you cover to cover,
Go and make people believe what you say is true,
Bear with your reader,
Don't let it go too far,
On no account be frightened to unlock your ideas.
Refuse to be the one who never gets read.
People laughing like nobody has before,
Where would you hide?
Protest against those with no imagination and creativity,
Create a new world where people have depth.
Yes, go book!
Celebrate the fact that everybody believes.
And above all, find the warmth of the people in the world!

Lorna Thomsen (12)
Cottenham Village College

My Poem Is . . .

My poem is emerald and gold and violet
My poem is small and beautiful and funny
My poem is strange and odd and amusing

My poem wants to help someone,
Someone who's not right
My poem does not want anyone to get hurt
In the world

My poem absolutely refuses to listen to
Anyone apart from the writer or the reader
My poem will never say no to anyone ever again

My poem tumbles over rocks like a brown bear
In the mountains
My poem flickers in the evening light like a shadow
That never wants to leave your side
My poem whispers like the wind, rustling the
Leaves on a tree in an empty village

My poem is like a hungry dog, always wanting more
My poem is like the Queen's jewels, precious and valuable
My poem is like the homely smell of your own house
My poem is for everyone!

Louise Thomas (12)
Cottenham Village College

Space Missions

Go ship, find the edge of time,
Go and seek the meaning of men,
Bear with you the hope of all life.

Do not give up hope and success.
Do not forget your purpose.
On no account do you lay yourself down.
On no account do you give up.

Refuse your feelings of distress.
Repudiate feelings of darkness.
Feelings of burning anger that fire
Through you like a scorching flame.
But they are extinguished with hope of your mind.

You dig through time and space.
Your journey will take you to a far, distant place.
Protest against evil and all that defies you.
Make your way through the depths of time
And create your own moment.

Celebrate the beginning of a moment
And share it with the hearts of people
And above all your work will be appreciated.
The Earth will ring your name,
So persist with evil and fight the darkness
And dreams will fly on aged wings.

Callum Fisher (12)
Cottenham Village College

My Poem Is . . .

My poem is white, red and black
My poem is dark, cruel and cold
My poem is shadowy, murderous and icy
My poem wants to drink your blood
And eat you alive, it wants death and Hell
My poem does not want happiness, joy, life and Heaven
My poem absolutely refuses the chance
Of a mortal life and to be loved
My poem glides and leaps like a ravenous werewolf
In the forest under the moon
My poem leaves you in darkness like the sun
Going to sleep on the horizon
My poem whispers like the trees in a lonely forest
My poem is like a witch's cat with glowing yellow eyes
My poem is like a ruby, bloody and crimson
My poem is for the shadows.

Sam Parker (12)
Cottenham Village College

Go Poem, Go . . .

Go poem, go to the poet you choose
Go and wriggle into little children's minds
Take their dreams, dive down; find the hearts and minds
of defenceless children
Do not turn back, complete your task.
Refuse their rejection; push your thoughts and dreams further
into their minds
Glide into the hearts, do not come out
Protest against all evil that tries to defeat you
Make people happy
Give laughter and seriousness to all people
Yes, go travel to many other people
Celebrate your victory
And above all do not give up
Follow your destiny.

Helena Did-dell (12)
Cottenham Village College

Spaceship

Go, ship, go to the edge of the universe
Go and take astronauts by complete surprise,
Take with you the thought of giving new facts
To anxious, learning school kids and scientist,
Bear with you the thought of failure and don't do it,
Carry with you the enthusiasm of all living creatures,
Do not disintegrate in the face of discovery,
Do not give up when failure strikes you down,
On no account crack under pressure of having
The weight of everyone's hope on your shoulders,
Refuse any will from inside that says go on give
Up you can't make it and you know it,
Dive into the black hole that is space like a man with
No fear and hopes of everything,
Make a last thrust at your goal and create a chance of success,
Give all of your enthusiasm, hope and desire to the
Young ones and fill their hearts and minds with inspiration,
Celebrate at the thought of making people who don't
Know a lot into kind, clever and normal people,
Yes, yes you've succeeded your mind is at rest and your
Thoughts deeper,
And above all you've made the world a much better place
With a spaceship to be inspired by,
Go, ship, go to the edge of the universe.

Ed Dimambro (12)
Cottenham Village College

Go Ship, Go

Go ship, go, far away, where nothing but a telescope can see you,
To the Milky Way.
Go and bring back what you have seen.
Take with you the proud and brave memories and dreams.
Do not be scared when you are alone.
Think how happy everyone will be when you return home.
On no account should you hesitate.
Refuse haste, don't quiver, be strong.
Jump like you weigh nothing, like you're floating without a cause.
Where no one can feel the force.
Protest against hate, don't feel angry if you fail.
Use it as an opportunity to learn.
Yes, go and conquer the solar system and live on it.
Celebrate the chance of a lifetime
And above all be proud of what you have experienced.

Jacqueline Mason (12)
Cottenham Village College

My Poem

My poem is red and black and blue
My poem wants to kill and steal
My poem does not want to get caught
My poem absolutely refuses to obey rules
My poem never listens to anybody
My poem stomps like a rhino through the African grasslands
My poem darkens the alleyways like a desperate criminal
My poem thunders through the streets like a terrible storm
My poem is like an angry lion hunting for its prey
My poem is like a battered cliff after a tremendous flood
My poem is like a tramp dying for food
My poem is for itself.

Peter Willey (12)
Cottenham Village College

Shadow In The Night

My poem is purple and orange and yellow,
my poem is extraordinary and brilliant and bold.

My poem is quality and happy and strange,
my poem does not want to leave your hands,
my poem absolutely refuses to be untold!

My poem creeps like a spider deep into your heart,
my poem has shadows like a stalker in the night,
my poem beats faster and faster like a heart at the centre of the Earth.

My poem is like a pouncing tiger hiding from its prey ready to attack,
it's like a setting sun gradually disappearing,
and like a beautiful rose bush growing and growing, getting bigger
then out flowers' colours: reds, whites and peachy oranges.

My poem is like one of the many precious stones of the world,
something to keep for a lifetime.

Rebecca Hawkes (12)
Cottenham Village College

My Poem Is . . .

My poem is red, green and silver
My poem is independent, small and fast
My poem wants to fly to the rings of Saturn
My poem does not want to crash land on the freezing
coldness of Pluto
My poem absolutely refuses to eat in a weird alien restaurant
on Jupiter
My poem will never give up
My poem glides invisibly through the city like a lonely man
My poem is silhouetted against the alleyways of a big city
leaving no trace
My poem makes no sound but leaves only the slight haze
of breath on a cold day
My poem is like the precious heart of the sea
My poem is like my cat, sneaky, a hunter but warm and cuddly
My poem is for anybody who wants to read it.

Matt McCreith (12)
Cottenham Village College

My Poem

My poem is gold and silver and bronze.
My poem is great and powerful and almighty.
My poem is funny and authentic and gleeful.
My poem wants fins like fish, to swim the green seas of land.
My poem doesn't want me to finish this poem.
My poem absolutely refuses to go to school.
My poem will never become boring.
My poem flies like a bird through the sky.
My poem shines like a star in the dark night.
My poem whispers like the wind through a quiet winter garden.
My poem is like a fox hunting stealthily through thickened forest.
My poem is like a treasure searched by pirates for years.
My poem is like a TV programme explaining itself.
My poem is like the smooth snow on top of a mountain in the Alps.
My poem is all of these and more!

Stefan Wolf (12)
Cottenham Village College

My Poem Is . . .

My poem is a dash of blue, a flick of white and a swirl of black,
My poem is swishing and violent and a frothing mist,
My poem is ferocious and a blackened hole,
My poem wants to move you, eat you and swallow you whole,
My poem does not want you to turn away
It wants you to be enhanced by its slow motion,
My poem absolutely refuses to be silent, behave or even listen,
My poem will never leave without a fight,
My poem sways like the rocking of the seesaw creaking softly in
                                                    the wind,
My poem glares as it forms a dark shadow,
My poem chants like the singing of a choir,
My poem is like a sleeping werewolf howling in the shine of the moon,
My poem is like the glinting of diamonds, rubies and sapphires,
My poem is like my garden, the rustling of leaves blowing in the wind,
My poem is for you, a picture I created.

Lauren Ryles (12)
Cottenham Village College

Go Book, Go

Go book, go book and fill the minds of lonely children.
Go and fill the world with adventure.
Carry with you words of wisdom from all over the world.
Do not be afraid to create life in darkened minds.
On no account be afraid of exploring the universe and fill it
with
inspiration.
Refuse to give up on children's imaginative minds.
Move around the Earth like a free soul and where shall you be
stopped!
Nowhere!
Protest against people giving up.
Create life in lonely souls all over the imaginative universe.
Yes go and fill empty mind with words of wisdom.
And above all *never* give up on your young apprentices.
Fill them with *hope*.

Tom Moller (12)
Cottenham Village College

My First Day

My first day . . .
Butterflies in my belly
Wobbling about like jelly
Nervous as I was I got lost
But I was boss.

Where to go I hadn't got a clue.
I looked like a fool
But I found my way only just.
I felt worried as dust.

On I went to lesson
Where to go I was guessing
Troubled what to do left me in a muddle
I felt as though I was in a puddle.

Sarah Cozens (15)
Cromwell Community College

The Fun You Can Have With Snow

When it's snowing
the river stops flowing
and people go ice skating

When it's snowing
it's always two feet
and when it happens
my dad is always asleep

When it's snowing
the people are throwing
snowballs at my face

When it's snowing
the people are making
snowmen beneath my feet

When it's snowing
the people are snowboarding
down the hill at top speed
then you hit a *tree.*

Thomas Collett (11)
Cromwell Community College

Kittens

Kittens' fur is so soft.
They walk so softly on and off,
They walk to the fire and curl up.
A little purr you can hear,
A day turns to night,
Not a kitten in sight.

Sophie Morton (11)
Cromwell Community College

House Matches

It's a ruthless life for the boys,
At this time of year it's horrible,
It's dangerous and it's war.

The time has come,
They've started, the match has begun.
They're like rhinos but with sticks.
Who's going to win? It's a mission,
A mission for popularity.
You wouldn't think it's so dangerous, would you?
I mean it's hockey, a game of fun,
A speaking, a civilised game
Or it as until the girls
At our school took over,
They're vicious and it's all
Because of *house matches*.

Phoebe Ladds (12)
Cromwell Community College

When The Wind Blows

As she moves quickly through the grass,
Without making a sound,
Swiftly through the wind she runs,
Brown covered in white spots,
As quiet as a mouse.
All in turn these feet of hers
Thump on the ground,
But then she runs faster than ever
Running like the wind.
She gradually slows down as she falls to the floor,
Blood everywhere but still no sound
As the wind blows around her,
All you can hear is the whistle of the wind
Blowing through the trees.

Sophie Butler-Honeybun (11)
Cromwell Community College

The Cold And Lonely Night

The moon up in the sky,
Shimmering its reflection in the cold river.
In the river you see the golden fishes,
Swimming slowly around.

You stare up into the sky,
You see the sparkling stars,
Sparkling, shining, glowing through,
The cold and lonely night.

Time goes by slowly,
As you look around,
Glancing, glancing,
But there is no sound.

You walk around,
You climb a tree,
To see the silver branches,
With the golden leaves.

The sun is now rising,
It is getting brighter,
You say goodbye to the night,
Until the day has done.

Charlie Dawson (11)
Cromwell Community College

The Waves

The sea is like a hungry dog,
With the sea splashing against the shore,
The sand sinks into the ground once again,
Beautiful sandcastles sit in the sun,
But then the waves wash them away,
Then some more appear.

Kayleigh Peacock (11)
Cromwell Community College

Dreams

As dreams go by day by day,
You can start to wonder if they come true,
At night I start dreaming as I lay
And each night my dreams are new.

I wonder whether I will be glad
And I wonder how I might die,
But I never dream about being sad,
Because my dreams might be a lie.

I dream about deep things,
Like how I might part
And I dream about the golden rings,
Around my beautiful heart.

But when my dreams come to a dawning,
I really, really don't like it,
I wake up to a beautiful morning
And just think, stare and sit.

Aimee Judge (11)
Cromwell Community College

Kittens

Kittens like to pounce and fight,
but really are a delight,
their delicate whiskers, pink little noses, round innocent eyes.
You're off to school and they're on their own *pounce!*
They're out of the box,
first to the kitchen,
knocking cups over, glass on the floor.
Running to the sitting room leaping on the curtains *rip!*
Scratching the sofa.
Back in the box and fast asleep.

Harriet Muller (11)
Cromwell Community College

Cunning Cat!

Cunning, cunning cat,
Crafty as a fox,
Sneaky as a snake,
Prowling through the darkness . . .
Getting ready to pounce!

3 . . . 2 . . . 1 . . .
And it leaps upon the tall, tall fence,
Silently it jumps down on next-door's patio,
Crawling along the dark floor, the dark, dark floor
Until it gets to next-door's pond.

The blackness of the water and reflection of the moon,
Tiny orange goldfish swimming, swimming *splash!*
In a sweep, two paws and it's hooked a fish.
Its scales glinting in the moonlight.
The cat drops it on the floor.
The fish wriggles, wriggles, wriggles.
In go the cat's teeth sinking, sinking in.
The fish stuck between his jaws.
The cat crawling along the dark, dark floor.

Cunning, cunning cat
Crafty as a fox.
Sneaking as a snake
Prowling through the darkness,
Getting ready to pounce!

Sheree Markham (11)
Cromwell Community College

A Little Girl In White

A pale little girl in white,
Walking all alone.
No one knows her name.
She looks around trying
To find a friend.

She thinks she is a puppet,
Everyone pulling her about.
She has no freedom,
She always wishes to be free
That little girl as white
As freshly fallen snow.

Some say she wished too hard,
Some say she wished too long,
But one morning,
They found she was gone.

Amie-Louise Bidwell (12)
Cromwell Community College

The Sea

The sea.
The storms,
They both come together to
Create something completely different,
Frightening weather tipping, turning
Rolling whatever lay upon it.

The fisherman's boat, cold and lonely,
Nowhere to go, nowhere to hide,
Nowhere to run.
All alone on the open sea,
Panicking, looking for somewhere to go
For somewhere to hide,
For somewhere to run.

Morgan Skipper (11)
Cromwell Community College

The Fenland Rexes

The Rexes are all mates,
They never worry about school or hot dates.
They concentrate on football,
The beautiful game on the pitch
To win the ball, you have to be nippy,
Like the golden Snitch.

There's Andy, Martin and Jonathan too,
Andy's mate Aaron, Div and Mike,
Are as tough as dried glue.
Spete's really cool, he's the best,
He'll run circles round the rest.

So the Fenland Rexes are all mates
And make a good team
They'll go up the tables like hot steam.
They can play in all sorts of weather,
So watch it! They'll have you at the end of your tether.
Fenland Rexes are all mates,
They never worry about school or hot dates!
(Much!)

Peter Loizou (13)
Cromwell Community College

Dolphins

D olphins leap through the waves
O ver and under splashing and crashing
L eaping and diving through the wind
P ractising for their famous tricks
H appy dolphins jumping up and down
I n and out the waves they dive
N obody can leap through the sky
S plashing happily they play and dive.

Donna Venni (12)
Cromwell Community College

Home 'Sweet' Home

I step into the building, the van speeds away
I'm all alone, the darkness spreading like fire
Why did I move? I should've stayed with my friend
I'm stuck in the tower block, 13 storeys from the ground.

The lift is broken, I have to walk
Other residents glare at me evily
I'm scared of heights, I can't go on!
I enter my flat and slam the door shut.

My boxed possessions loom eerily above me
I step into my bedroom, the silence is screaming
I leap under the covers without getting undressed
I shut my eyes from the world of strangers . . .

I hear a creak in the hall . . .
I sit up in a flash . . .
I want to scream but my throat is clenched in fright
I hear a pounding on the door . . .

They're coming
They're beating down the door
They're coming for me
I can't escape.

Victoria Bailey (12)
Cromwell Community College

The Sun Is Setting In The Sky

The sun is setting in the sky
Everybody say goodbye,
As the sun sets you say goodnight
Because here comes darkness to replace the sun
The moon comes out shining and sparkling
In the night sky what a wonderful sight
To look forward to.

Nicola McDermott (11)
Cromwell Community College

Football Is A Shame

Football is a nasty game,
All the spitting and all the shame,
People sliding all over the place,
Smack! There goes a stud in the face,
Bang! There goes that stupid whistle,
Peter and Andy start to tussle,
The manager of all the team,
Comes in and starts to scream,
'You lot were rubbish out there,
It was as if I was in a nightmare.'
Bang! It is part two
And all the players slide like glue.
It is the second half,
And I, the manager, start to laugh.
'You're all rubbish,' they hear,
'Relegation is what I fear.'
So I walked off in a bunch of tears,
The fans were booing along with cheers.
As I walked off in a foul mood,
All the points gobbled up like food
And that's the end of this silly game,
I told you football is a shame.

Martin Lawrence (12)
Cromwell Community College

Love

Love is something that never
Can be replaced.

It's always in your heart,
Whatever you do,
It's always with you.

It stays locked in your memory forever.

Jasetta Hood (12)
Cromwell Community College

Deadly Rainbow

Red is anger. The red of a rag
makes a bull angry.

Orange is gluttony. The orange of chocolate
makes men gluttonous.

Yellow is envy. The yellow of the sun
makes men envious of the gods.

Green is greed. The green of the grass
makes me greedy for land.

Blue is sloth. The blue of the waves
makes men lazy.

Indigo is lust. The indigo of Neptune
makes men lust for the stars.

Violet is blasphemy. The violet-blue
of bad language is blasphemous.

Carl Turpie (12)
Cromwell Community College

My Step!

Step 1, 2, 3
What am I doing?
Step 1, 2, 3
Why are people booing?
Step 1, 2, 3
What am I doing wrong?
Step 1, 2, 3
There goes the gong.
Step 1, 2, 3
My time is up
Step 1, 2, 3
I have a feeling I didn't win the dancing cup.

Hannah Christmas (12)
Cromwell Community College

The Living Blue!

What could I be?
I'm living in the sea,
I'm blue and ready for you!
I splash at you!
I go over you!
Which makes babies go, 'Boo-hoo.'
Some people don't like me, some people do
I've got a best friend, his name is Loo
You won't know him, he won't know you
Now come on down we're ready for you.
I flow over Earth, I flow over you
I get cleaned up and I come out of taps for you.
You don't like me
What could I be?
Oh yeah I am the - sea.

Bianca Parmenter (13)
Cromwell Community College

Sea Girl

The waves splash and crash against the cliff's edge
Violent on this very cold, chilling day.

The currents began picking up as a little girl, cold and bare,
Walked across the stones and shells which cut her little feet.

There was no one to be seen except the little girl
With waves towering over her.
She looked like a ghost walking to the crazy waves.

A young boy was shouting to the girl, 'Stop!' but she wouldn't
She was dragged towards the waves and never seen again.

Sarah McAdie (12)
Cromwell Community College

Love!

Love is like a liquid swimming
Through my body.
No headlights or policemen to
Stop it when it's in a hurry.
But when it's broken it can
Be like a self-destructive grenade.
But my feelings for this one true boy
Are irritable and insane.
So help me now for
I'm in a twisted emotion,
There is water breaking from
My window souls and they
Have nowhere else to go.
For I am now all alone,
Because when eviction day
Comes to me, I have nothing
Else to live for. This one true
Love lives forever and more.

Sarah Snow (13)
Cromwell Community College

The Stray

The stray, scruffy dog lay down to rest,
With a wound on his paw and a scar on his chest.
He looked so helpless lying there
Everyone walked by as if they didn't care.

Then along came a girl whose name I don't know,
She was very little swaying to and fro.
She looked over at the wreck and walked over to the dog,
Just to check. The girl picked up the dog,
And walked home disappearing into the fog.

Joanna Turton (12)
Cromwell Community College

The Race

The starter had his arm held high,
The time stood still,
The crowds seemed to vanish,
Silence echoed throughout the stadium,
I was poised and ready to go,
Bang!
I was off like a speeding bullet,
The only sound was the dull thud
Of my feet upon the emerald-green grass
And the occasional cheer from the watching crowd,
The finishing line came into view,
With a final burst of energy I was there,
The ear-splitting noise of the crowds returned,
I had won the race!

Francesca Millard (12)
Cromwell Community College

A Day Of Motorcross

We pull up, I quickly rush out, 'Hurry Dad, hurry.'
I'm running round and around, in and out.
It's finally down, I jump and shout,
Start it, rev it, ride up and down.
It is like a person has taken the Earth
And put it in the freezer, it is that cold out here.
I can't feel my fingers but it doesn't stop me though.
I go around a corner and over a jump,
Go on the speed track and quickly pull away.
Chasing a person all the way down the straight,
I get my chance but it goes wrong
My wheel slips out.
I go skidding along the sloppy floor
Tree right ahead! I know this is the *end! Aarrgghh!*

Jacob Cavilla (12)
Cromwell Community College

Rid Me Of This Pain!

Jealousy,
The anger welling up inside me.
I stand, I stare.
Lord, please, rid me of this pain.

The whole world is against me,
If only I could be him.
I stand, I stare,
Lord, please, rid me of this pain.

Look at them, there,
Swarming around, talking about me.
I stand, I stare,
Lord, please, rid me of this pain.

How I wish I could be with them,
Laughing and joking too,
I stand, I stare,
Lord, please, rid me of this pain.

Yet the gap is so small, but so agonisingly final,
The fine line between greatness and insanity
And so, in the face of adversity, I must,
I must show them that I can.

And Lord, please
If you hear me,
I beg you,
Rid me of this pain!

Matthew Barnes (12)
Cromwell Community College

Jealousy Has Come To Haunt Me

Walking down the street that day,
Was weird in some kind of way,
I used to walk here with my friend,
A tear rolled own my cheek.
Now she's off with another friend,
Jealousy has come to haunt me.

Why couldn't I just nod my head and wave?
Instead of crying in the rain.
The pain is hard,
I have nobody else.
Jealousy has come to haunt me.

I'm OK,
I'll get through this,
Someday I wish.
Maybe she'll come back some day,
Jealousy has come to haunt me,
Forever!

Kelly Stephens (12)
Cromwell Community College

A Turtle

Movement that is me
Over and over you will see
Very green that is me
Every day you see me on the sand
Many of you lend a hand
Very thankful you understand
Even though I'm very slow
Nothing will stop the way I go
A sea turtle is what I am
So now do you understand?

Nikaela Walton (13)
Cromwell Community College

The Nessy Hunter

Early morning,
Slip out of the house.
Take backpack,
Put a rope, an apple, a camera and a torch in,
Run down the path,
Head for Loch Ness,
Look at the deep, dark water,
Shine a torch,
Can't see anything or anyone,
Start to lower myself down one of the hills surrounding the loch,
Must get to the bottom.
Look for the monster,
I'll be famous,
Drop the apple,
It rolls down the hill,
Splash!
The sound echoes all around,
The torch goes out,
All alone in the dark,
A dark shape rises from the lake,
Snaky neck,
Grab camera,
Take a picture,
Flash!
The flash spooks the creature,
It lights up his eyes,
An ear-splitting scream,
Which one of us dies?

Holly Gladwin (13)
Cromwell Community College

Would Thou Break Under Pressure?

Would thou break under pressure?
If all in the world was covered,
Covered in the darkness of death.
Would thou break?

If the covered crows at mornings come,
If the wind howls in foul smells
And when all turn to your council,
Would thou break?

Silence falls, darkness comes,
All creations faltered.
The heart of the world in your grasp.
Would thou break?

In a senseless place where dreams are muffled,
Muffled by the ear-piercing scream of children.
Where art the crime of passion?
Passion for life.
No one cares for the worries of the elders,
Mountains, Earth, sea, sand,
All results of time.
So when pressure builds,
Our hearts brought to strain,
Think not of the living who are pretentious,
But of the unheard cries of people who crumble.
Crumble under pressure
When the world turns rotten
And fate takes its last breath,
You're alone with no one to help you,
Would thou break?

Daniel Upton (12)
Cromwell Community College

Monkeys

Monkeys are funky,
Monkeys are cool,
Monkeys are cheeky
And that's not all.

Monkeys are hairy,
Monkeys are sweet,
Monkeys are human-like
With their little hands and feet.

Monkeys are funny,
Monkeys are cute,
Monkeys are clever,
They could play a flute.

Monkeys are cuddly,
Monkeys are ape,
Monkeys are mischievous,
They're all a different shape.

To sum it all up, monkeys are fun
And given the chance, I would have one.

Michele Smalley (13)
Cromwell Community College

Wind, Friend Or Foe?

Wind is as delicate as a silk cloth
Or rougher than sandpaper
Wind can decide the weather
Or even the state of a person.

Wind can be a friend or foe
We'll never know
But until we do
Wind is with us for evermore
Graciously keeping us
And everything else alive.

Ben Robinson (12)
Cromwell Community College

Weather

Falling
slowly on my
red car
looks like we
won't be
travelling
far!

The
sun's
peeping
through the
clouds,
the snow has
stopped
altogether
now!

I can
finally
go on that
day out,
'Yippee' the
children all
laugh and
shout!

Natalie Rayner (13)
Cromwell Community College

Monsters

Monsters are fat,
Monsters are thin,
Monsters are ugly,
They live in bins.

Watch out kids,
They like to eat you,
They gobble you up
And don't even chew.

There is a monster
Who is a thief,
Big and smelly
With long sharp teeth.

He'll steal your dinner
He'll steal your tea
I hope the monster
Doesn't come near me.

They walk, they jump,
They run and skip.
They can move so fast,
They are really quick.
But some are big
And move real slow,
But they are still scary
And you should know!

Joanne Pryke (13)
Cromwell Community College

Hunting

Creeping in the grass
Being as quiet as he can
Shh! As he gets nearer to his prey
Pounce!
Run as fast as a cheetah
Oh I forgot I am just that
Got it? Yes! Now I can eat
Ripping it to pieces
Tearing it apart
Mmm! That was nice
Now I'll find somewhere to sleep.

Briony Payne (13)
Cromwell Community College

The Sky

The sky is black and grey tonight,
With the stars twinkling up above
The moon peeped through
The sky got light
I stared at the sky hoping and wishing
That everything would be alright.

Kyrstie Watkins (14)
Cromwell Community College

Love Is . . .

L ove is hanging around together
O n the beach and around the shops
V iewing sights and everywhere
E ating and drinking together

I n and out all the time
S weet dreams, sweetheart.

Sandra Lacey (13)
Cromwell Community College

Windy Weapons

A spear through the heart
Which flies like a dart
An arrow through the foot
Which needs a look.
A swing of an axe
Which slides like wax
A slash from a sword
Because you can't run like a lord
A shot from a gun
So you run for your mum.

Daniel Reeve (13)
Cromwell Community College

The Wind

You know you can feel it,
You can hear it,
But you can't see it,
It's the weather,
It's very clever.

It's always doing something,
Its sounds can be thought to be something else,
When it's hot it can bring coldness to the world.

Joshua Grant (12)
Cromwell Community College

Snails

M oving like a snail
O n the tip of the tail;
T iny, slowly as can be
I n there is a stinging bee
O n the tree it goes
N o one even knows.
   Ssshhh!

Carly Harrison (13)
Cromwell Community College

My Family

M y family's mad and wild
Y ou always see them smiling

F amily's always there for you
A rguments hardly happen
M ade to love me
Y ou'd love a family like mine
I love them so much
L oving, caring and kind
Y ou want my family?

Josie Paynter (13)
Cromwell Community College

Hungry

There was once a boy called Peter,
Who was starving with nothing to eat.
He went to the corner shop for something sweet,
But there was nothing he wanted to eat.
He wanted something that he could heat,
So he went to the butcher for some meat
And that was perfect to eat.

Chris Chambers (13)
Cromwell Community College

Dancing

The stage is lit
The audience awaits
Proud parents clap
As they smile with glee
Children point, 'Look at me,'
And that's why I love
My dancing.

Kirsty Earl (13)
Cromwell Community College

Football

The moist, wet grass twinkles
In the light,
The music blares out loud,
The game is about to begin.

For a minute,
Everything grinds to a halt.
Everybody is frozen in time.
Suddenly, like an explosion,
The footballers spring out
Like cannonballs from a cannon.

As the game starts,
The footballers get ready.
In a flash of lifetime,
The goal has been scored.

Nicola Compton (13)
Netherhall School

The Girl

Heart beats slower and slower.
'Ha ha,' girls laughing.
A tear rolls down her face.
No hand on her shoulder.
Nobody there.
A slam of the door, the sound of her running down the corridor.
Nee naw, goes the police car.
Everywhere you look you can see search parties.
Two days later.
A black car, black hats and suits.
A hole in the ground, now full of sorrow.
Everyone walks away.
This is the point that *they* stop laughing.

Rachel Kurdynowska (13)
Netherhall School

Sundown

The sun melts away behind the mountains,
Leaving rays of red and orange light,
Like melted strawberry and orange ice cream.

Down it goes,
Slowly,
Slowly vanishing.

A bright circle appears in the night above,
The moon,
Lighting up the dark world around us.

The stars,
Pop up like popcorn popping in a microwave,
Shattering the sky with bright light.

One by one the planets appear,
Squeezing through each star,
Trying to find a space.

Flashing lights zoom across the night,
As aeroplanes speed off,
Into the distance.

Philippa Joslin (13)
Netherhall School

Fishing

The rod goes back
and forward,
and back,
until the perfect cast is made.

The hook and bait lie waiting,
bobbles with impatience,
although still worried.

The water becomes unsettled.
Fish are near,
the hook and bait still waiting.

Bang!

The daring one snatches the bait,
tugging and tugging,
but further inland it is pulled.

The fish pulled until visible,
the net is used
for the perfect collection.

Ashley Meadows (13)
Netherhall School

The Night Of The Eagle

He flew from the branch,
Gliding in the dark night air,
Wings spread like the wind.

Into the darkness,
Keeping watch with his black eyes,
It was his forest.

Guarding the forest,
Omnipotent skymaster,
The moon as his torch.

His shadow is blue,
Like the dark velvet mole fur,
One of his subjects.

His misty eyes scan
Over the treetops that are,
His wonderful land.

Deep in his wise eyes
You can see the sad sorrow
As another dies.

It did not suffer,
But died in its peaceful sleep,
Its spirit has gone.

So ends a good life,
The fox shall be remembered,
Its family grieves.

He lands on the branch,
Another night's patrol done,
Now is time for sleep.

Animals will come,
The morning will bring them all,
For the funeral.

Mark Yao (13)
Netherhall School

An Innocent Sweet
(This poem is about the unnecessary use of gelatine in sweets)

The sweet sits on the table in front of me
A mute witness
To a terrible cruelty*

The key to a strange life
That I
Have never known

The surface white and spotted
Freshly fallen snow
Or a deadly disease?

Green fades to white like an apple,
The inside and the outside
Lurid and garish

At first touch the surface is rough and grainy
But underneath it is elastic, rubbery,
Fake

I sniff the sweet, it is
Chemical
And artificial

I'm not eating it, my friend is
I can image the taste though,
Over-sweet and artificial

And then a nasty aftertaste,
A lingering taste of what is underneath,
This is how I imagine it

In my head I hear the jingle:
'Kids and grown-ups love it so
the happy world of Haribo'

And underneath I hear the screaming of animals,
The dark history
Of a seemingly innocent sweet.

Jasmine Wingfield (12)
Netherhall School

The Sailing Ship

A big sailing ship
Sails out of the large harbour
Starting its voyage

The boat leaves the calm
Into the stormy waters
The wind whips the sails

Folks are on the quay
The crew look back wistfully
Their new life beckons

The ship's golden aura
It is a symbol of hope
In a bleak, dark land

It is a new ship
The trees' wisdom is in it
Guiding it forward

The ocean's huge roar
Frightening the tiny ship
And pushing it back

The salty sea breeze
Pushing the sailing ship
On its long journey.

Mark Streather (13)
Netherhall School

The Haribo Crocodile Sonnet

I sit here looking at this noxious sweet,
The artificial colours make me gag.
It's full of gelatine, I don't eat meat,
My teacher pulls another from its bag.
I pick it up, it's grainy, just like sand,
Fluorescent green against a bed of white.
It sits there like a dog toy in my hand,
I'm sure that I would vomit with one bite.
Inside my head the jingle starts to play,
'Kids and grown-ups love it so!' *Oh no!*
It's started now, it'll never go away,
No freedom from the world of Haribo.
And if this croc were living would it moo?
How many cows were boiled to make this chew?

Lilith Cooper (12)
Netherhall School

Dawn Of A New Day

The sun glances over the horizon,
Throwing a veil of mist
Across the land,
And a paint palette of colour
Is spilled across the sky.

Your tongue picks up every taste;
The sweetness of the sun,
The bitterness of the wind.
Every sense prickles a little
And you turn your face to the sky.

The birdsong drifts over the hill,
The constant buzz of life
Creating a layer of music,
Echoing around the world,
Waking those who choose to hear . . .

Eloise Jenkins (11)
St Mary's School, Cambridge

Homeless

I'm sitting by this cold, hard wall,
Thinking, *why is life so cruel?*
Why do people pass me by?
Embarrassed to look me in the eye
Do they think I like it where I am?
Think it's all just one big scam
Or that I've lost it on the drink?
Yeah, that's what some working people think
But most of them don't mean to be,
Nasty, cruel and to ignore me,
In their own little worlds they hurry past,
No time to stop, time goes too fast
They hardly notice that I'm there,
No time for me, none to spare.
For a homeless man sleeping on the street,
I'm just one of the many they meet,
They think one of us is just like the rest
Give some money to one, yeah they've done their best,
They gave a bit, to one down the lane,
No more to give and it's starting to rain,
So they don't stop and help, just hurry on by,
As the clouds that are forming obscure the sky,
They wouldn't be dismissive if they know the way,
I live on the streets every night and each day,
They wouldn't look disgusted, when I clutch at their hem,
If they thought that one day, this could be them.

Sheri Brown (14)
St Mary's School, Cambridge

You Can't Be That

I told them
When I grow up
I'm not going to be a dentist
Or someone that runs for money
No, I'm going to eat bananas and sneeze
I'm going to be a chimpanzee

I told them
When I grow up
I'm not going to be an actor,
A teacher or on TV
No going from door to door is for me
I guess a salesman I shall be

My parents don't understand me
I'll be a snake slithering through the leaves
I'll be a monkey climbing up the trees
They do not realise I can fill any desire
They do not realise I can walk through fire.

Matthew Ellis (11)
Sawston Village College

The Dark

The moonlight shines.
The dark grow bigger.
The still silent trees stare.
As I lie in my bed scared.
The dreary clouds fill the sky.
The secret box lets out all ghosts.
The dark is in the world of its own.

Shaun Poulter (12)
Sawston Village College

Chocolate

When you're feeling down and a little blue,
A piece of chocolate is the perfect thing for you,
As the smell drifts up your nose,
All your troubles sink down to your toes.

There's a huge variety of bars to choose,
From Snicker to Mars and toffee chews,
There's only one problem and this is it,
You have to have more than just one little bit.

Once you start gobbling it's hard to stop,
And soon you've gobbled up the whole shop,
You start to feel sick and then run to the loo,
All your troubles start flooding back to you,

So next time you catch sight of a chocolate eclair,
Limit yourself to one little square!

Sophie Graham (13)
Sawston Village College

Alone

Homeless is when you're on your own,
Cold with nothing to hold on to,
No happy memories of childhood,
Begging for scraps and food,
People looking at you differently,
Like you're a pile of rubbish
That they're higher than you.

In the same clothes day after day,
Sleeping in the wet windy streets,
Wrapping yourself in the same smelly rag,
An empty belly when you go to sleep and wake up,
Homeless is when you're alone.

Stacey Attwood (12)
Sawston Village College

Night

The sound of the dustbin lid,
Rattling in the wind, clanking on the bricks,
The dog's barking sends a chill down my spine,
As I see the shadow of the burglar that hid.

The icy squeaks of the rats in the street,
Eating the leftover pizzas and chips
And scrabbling at the bin bags sprawled around,
Sitting in the car, staring out, I sweat in the heat.

As the old oak trees sway in the breeze
And the odd car comes down the road,
I can't hear anything,
But then the burglar falls to his knees.

Then suddenly a flash of blue,
A flash of light, a squeal of a siren,
A couple of shouts and all are gone,
Then all you can see is a full moon.

Jessica Woodward (12)
Sawston Village College

Nightmare

I was hot and sticky
With a bush fire crackling in the background
The boy from next door,
Rhys,
Screaming out loud
So, out of bed I crept,
And,
Oh no I saw what was wrong
A big greedy goblin was,
Now eating me ali . . .

Russell Boatman (12)
Sawston Village College

Friendships

I am always by myself,
But nobody seems to care.
I have no friends, no not one,
It's as if I'm never there.

But who needs friends,
It certainly can't be me,
My best friend has been taken,
Oh well, let it be.

I'm used to being on my own,
A single static bolt.
It shouldn't really be like this,
Maybe it's all my fault.

To take away my friendship,
Is a really awful crime.
But to carry on and bully me,
Now is not the time.

I don't know what to do about it,
They've made it crystal clear.
I'm never meant to be one of them,
I'll just live my life in fear.

My pride has definitely gone for good,
I know it won't be back.
The only thing I can do now,
Is get my life back on track.

Kerry Sayer (12)
Sawston Village College

This Is My Life

I live my life in this small metal cage,
I'm poked at and prodded,
I work for no wage.

Why is it me that goes through such pain?
All these humans look at me,
What can they gain?

I have injections and needles stuck in my side,
There is nothing I can do,
There's nowhere to hide!

They expect me to be happy trapped in this place,
When they knock on my cage,
I put on a brave face.

I'm really quite gloomy not happy at all,
Poor little me,
So weak and so small.

It seems I must suffer so that men can be well
The more I'm tested on,
The more drugs they sell.

If you saw me you would understand,
That my life is a misery,
I need a helping hand!

Jessica Ashby (12)
Sawston Village College

We Will Remember Them!

You see the poppies pinned on shirts
And wonder what they're for!
You never think of those who fought,
In that long-lost war.
These fighters they did fight for you,
For their country they did die,
But now they're all but forgotten,
For the lives of many no one still does cry.

Do not forget their bravery
As they fought for you
Even though they're gone from Earth,
They still have feelings too!

Bravery is dashed, all hope is diminished,
When you turn to war,
Held together only by, that all important promise,
The promise to serve your country, till you can no more.

Do not forget their bravery
As they fought for you.
Even though they're gone from Earth,
They still have feelings too!

Today our lives are busy, but it does not take much time,
To remember those who died
And saved our country fine.
So stop and give a moment,
To those who gave their lives
No matter what they did for us,
Be sure their memory survives.

Victoria Brown (15)
Sawston Village College

Silly Old Baboon

There was a baboon
Who, one afternoon,
Said, 'I think I will fly to the sun.'
So, with two great palms,
Strapped to his arms
He started his take-off run.

Mile after mile,
He galloped in style
But never once left the ground.
'You're running too slow,'
Said a passing crow,
'Try reaching the speed of sound.'

So he put on a spurt -
By God how it hurt.
Sprinting through the night,
Both his knees caught alight
And smoke billowed from his rear
And there were great clouds of steam.

The silly old baboon
Flew past the moon
And waved hello to Mars
And there he saw plenty of cars.
As he flew past Venus,
He saw his girlfriend, Teenus.

PS He got to the sun
And had an unfortunate death.

Joshua Ansell (11)
Sawston Village College

Night Poem

The warm beer foamed a white moustache on the stranger's face
As his tall looming figure stoops into the bustling pub.
The street lamps emit a warm glow and the moon rises high
Into the air like a silver god looking forth upon his land.
There is a commotion on Mill Street, what is it?
It is a poor homeless person
Being stolen from, what little money he has.
This land is bad.
All of a sudden a huge fiery face appears in the sky
And a long arm sweeps the area.
There is a terrific battle between the sun and the moon.
In one horrible strike, the moon is banished from its evil kingdom.
The usual hubbub erupts in the sunlit street,
People go to work, come back.
Then the moon rules again.

Nicholas Willoughby (12)
Sawston Village College

Who Am I?

I follow my leader wherever he goes,
Although not when it's dark,
I seem to be scared, so I run away,
Run far away, until morning begins.

I copy my leader whatever he does,
He runs, he skips, I always keep up with him,
But sometimes the cloud covers the light,
I'm nowhere to be seen.

I watch over my leader whenever he moves,
He cries, I'll always look up to him,
No matter what he does I'll always follow him.

Ross MacIntyre (11)
Sawston Village College

Anger

Is a volcano erupting,
A pot of red paint,
A bomb about to go off,
A pirate's headscarf,
A tornado destroying everything in sight,
A terrorist,
A meteor crashing into the Earth,
A star exploding,
A Chinese dragon,
A
Sin
A
Sin
A
Sin.

Alex Stratton (12)
Sawston Village College

Who Am I?

I bear cold weather
and dish out colds.
I change the colour of the leaves on the trees
and bring big winds.
I turn the world white
and can solidify water.
I bring Father Christmas and a happy new year.

Who am I?

I am winter!

David Cousins
Sawston Village College

Why Can't I Be Loved?

Where am I?
In my bed,
I don't know,
Where should I be?
On the table,
That's where I am,
All battered and torn,
Held by the scruff,
Why can't I be loved?
By my owner,
Why? Why? Why?
I want to have fun,
Playing with my owner.

Paul Munden (11)
Sawston Village College

My Blanket Cat

Soft and cuddly, up to my cheek,
Woollen with your satin chic,
Here to comfort me, listen to me moan,
I never, ever want to be on my own.

I took you everywhere; nursery, town,
I once took you to see a clown,
Come on now get to bed,
Things are whirring inside my head.

As I grew older I started to forget,
Then I got my really cute pet.
My ginger little pussy cat,
Soft and cuddly asleep on the mat.

Catherine McMullan (11)
Sawston Village College

Darkness

A night-time hunter
King of black holes
Never near torches, candles and raging fire
And always reborn at dusk

A silent cloak
The owl's domain
Seeking for corners, caves and moonless nights
But never alive at dawn

A silent assassin
Killed by, but killing light
Ruler of space, but never near stars
Born again, every 24.

Martin Rolph (12)
Sawston Village College

Death

I am a gloomy shadow that hovers in unlit places,
I am an icy breeze that is never far away,
I am the most feared thing in life,
I am a huge black wave that takes over everything,
I am a thick grey fog, which lingers in gloomy streets,
I am a small part of everyone but can take over extremely fast,
I am the last thing you see,
I am with you forever,
I am always around,
I am death!

Charlotte Downing (12)
Sawston Village College

You Can't Be That!

I told them
When I grow up
I'm not gonna be a biologist or a pilot
No! I will live as long as an old folks' tale
I'm gonna be a big blue whale.

They said I couldn't be that
They didn't even believe me

So I told them
When I grow up
I'm not gonna be a policeman or a fireman
A milkman or a lawyer
No! I'm gonna live in hot conditions
I will hunt an antelope called Brian
I'm gonna be a lion

They said I couldn't do that
They didn't even believe me

They don't understand me,
So I'll be a vulture smelling rotten meat
Or I'll be a racoon's nose sniffing out a treat
They don't even realise I can fulfil any desire
They don't even realise among them walks a raging fire.

Scott Lansdale (11)
Sawston Village College

Going Nowhere

In my bed I sit not looking towards tomorrow
My head throbs,
The pain would not go away.
I am in a whirlpool with nobody to talk to.
As if they never notice, they ignore.
I keep fighting for my rights.
Ah ha, as if I would go anywhere!
But now I hope tomorrow never comes.

If I get knocked out
I bet death would be good.
Sugar trees they must have,
That's better than my bully,
Who never sleeps or rests,
Her ever so strong anger,
She keeps in her head.
As they say tomorrow must come.
As for me I know I am not going nowhere!

Pamela Akita
Sawston Village College

Fire

A fierce beast.
A hungry lion trying to catch its food.
A kettle steaming.
A hot sun.
A roaring volcano letting off sparks.
Black bats flying around everywhere
Scratching and clawing your body like a knife
Stabbing you.
The colours of hell
What am I?
Fire.

Annie Whyte (11)
Sawston Village College

Nightmare And Sleep!

N ightmares
I n the night
G hosts, ghouls
H idden sprites
T ime-travelling
M onsters screech
A ttacking us all
R oaring beast, then
E xciting nightmare, entering
S leep.

S leeping shadows,
L eaping stars,
E njoying and relaxing,
E ntering Mars,
P illow soft, then you're awake,
I n half consciousness
N othing can stay
G oing, going, gone and you're awake.

Jade Field (12)
Sawston Village College

What Am I?

A man's beard,
Trees' winding fingers,
Blazing light,
Mad over matches.
A hissing snake in danger,
Crackling dramatically like a firework in action.
Danger if you touch its steaming body,
Heat provider.
I spread quicker than butter over bread.

Kate Turner (11)
Sawston Village College

The Night's Adventure (Storm Over Our Tent)

I lay there listening
Waiting for it to end
You could hear it coming
Coming fast
It came from the sea
Faster and faster it ran
Across the beach
And up the cliff
To our tent
Where it would stay to play
Shaking the tent again and again
I could feel its breath
Rush across my face
I could hear the rain
Above my head
It seemed to last forever
I lay there listening
Waiting for it to end.

Alice Tasker (12)
Sawston Village College

Fire

A thousand licking tongues.
The crackling of a paper bag.
The colours of the sun at midday.
Infinite dancing bodies.
A scorching monster.
The murderer of wood.
Anger unleashed.
Fire.

Rowan Austin (11)
Sawston Village College

What Am I?

A spitting cobra
An inferno of flames
The helper of the Devil
A pack of roaring panthers
Death!
A pair of snarling jaws ready to swallow
A twister destroying everything in its way
A boiling knife slicing through a corpse
Razor-sharp teeth ripping you apart
A door to Hell.

Josh Pateman (12)
Sawston Village College

Midnight

House lights flicking on and off,
Dodgy looking people around with an occasional laugh,
Most people walking around this late,
Usually walk with at least one mate,
Except me, I'm all alone,
That's why I hold tight to my mobile phone,
It's very wet,
Makes scarier people come out I'd bet,
Out here it's raining cats and dogs
And nights around here aren't without fogs,
Stars and moon barely twinkling in the sky,
I have a funny feeling that I'm going to die.

Luke Tancock (12)
Sawston Village College

The Night's Secret

Rosy-cheeked children lay warm in their beds,
Not knowing that beyond their houses excited animals
Create a world of their own,
Fighting,
Talking,
Proudly strutting up and down the deserted street,
Waiting for dawn to break
When they quickly vanish out of human sight.
When the sun emerges over the trees,
The street appears untouched, spotless
Just like the humans left it.
They will never know the secret of the night.

Claire Green (12)
Sawston Village College

Night!

The black sky was there,
The stars and moon with the mist,
The sounds kept on coming.

The bird flew past me,
I couldn't catch a glimpse of it,
The trees kept on speaking.

I saw a shadow,
It came closer and closer,
It paused and was still.

I stayed up that night,
The noises kept on coming,
I laid asleep, night!

Nicola Slater (12)
Sawston Village College

A Frosty Night

Twisting and turning in my old creaky bed,
Not getting to sleep is something I dread.
I get up and go downstairs,
'Ouch,' I just had to trip over that bear!
I open the door to go outside,
There's my cat, she's trying to hide.
The big glowing moon is getting near
And the sky is so very, very clear.
In the distance is the silent motorway,
Here in my garden I'd love to stay.
The flickering, twinkling lights are fairies,
The everlasting field is very scary.
I walk along the crispy grass, crunch, crunch, crunch,
Whilst the little hedgehogs go munch, munch, munch!
Oh, how I would love to stay in my garden forever,
I better not because I don't like the cold weather.

Lucy Goodchild (13)
Sawston Village College

Midnight Scare

It was midnight,
This was a beautiful sight,
But then I saw a mystery shadow,
It looked like my friend Jackow,
I called his name,
There was a scream of pain,
I stood there with a scared look,
But, then I saw a big sharp hook,
It came closer and closer,
Then it was only my old ripped *poster*.

Katie Sinclair (12)
Sawston Village College

Getting Home

Running down the road
I'm scared
Toot-toot oh it's only an owl
Must get home
It isn't safe
Then out of the bush
Comes an old man
He attacked me with his walking stick
Must get home
I see my house
The light is on but I'm not there
Who is there?
I walk through the door
And I see . . .

David Phillips (13)
Sawston Village College

Night!

The moon shines in the sky,
While people still walk by.
The owls hoot on top of the tree,
When I walk past they look down at me.
The stars sparkle in the night,
As I can see a little mouse in sight.
Night can be a scary place to be,
Not a place people wish to be.
As the leaves rustle as they blow,
Someday it might even snow.
As owls go flying by,
Up, up in the dark sky.

Melanie Carder (12)
Sawston Village College

The Night's Story

The shivering shadows wobble in the wind,
Quivering quietly quacking in the wood,
The gormless grey ghosts gape in the house,
I stand still and scared, shaking.
My face is fixed with fear,
The stars shining, the moon is bright,
The sky has some light on this darkened night,
As the sun burns up the night burns out.
This is how my night works out.

Stacey Kemp (12)
Sawston Village College

Man In The Moon

When I look up at the moon and space
All I can think about is a man and his face
He stares down at us with a face bright and kind
You can stare back, he doesn't mind
When you're awake he always sleeps
A picture of you he always keeps.

Daniel Case (12)
Sawston Village College

Feelin' Weak

I thought I was powerful, I mean as a mountain and all,
But night and day is so much stronger.
Darkness is a bully,
It fights the sun every day; and it wins.
It must cheat surely? The sun is so powerful.
It seriously is a bully swallowing the clouds.
Sometimes I wish I was taller so I could help the sun
I am so much shorter being 4000 foot one.

Kyle Grainger (12)
Sawston Village College

The Night

Dark, not totally,
the moon and small stars
light the sky, sounds
are more noticeable
as there is an eerie silence
about the night, cold
a chilling wind, that whistles
and the cry of tomcats.

Shannesse Lane (12)
Sawston Village College

The Night Sea

As the cool sea hits against the rocks,
The stars reflect in the cool blue water,
The tide taken over the beach,
The sound of no one, just the roaring sea,
Shadows making faces in the gentle waves,
As the night draws in.

Zoey Demartino (12)
Sawston Village College

Night

The street lamp flickers.
A tramp living under a pile of boxes,
Shouting coming from closing pubs,
The shadows hiding them.
Muggers waiting for the perfect chance,
Their weapons ready to strike.

Nathan Whitaker (12)
Sawston Village College

Night

Night, is it far?
Night, is it icy?
Night, is it loneliness?
Night, is it the time to listen?
Night, is it the time to watch?
Night, is it death?
Night, is it life?
Night, is it the time to be alone?
Night, is it the time to be with friends and family?
Night, is it the beginning?
Night, is it the end?
Night, what is night?
Night is what you want it to be.

Lucas Reali (12)
Sawston Village College

The Night

The starry night sky,
Fades as gloomy clouds come,
Then strangeness occurs,
Until the rising sun.

Darkness of the night
Swirls to the break of dawn,
Before the morning light,
The cry of a baby being born.

The cold wind,
Lurks around the night,
Down back alleys,
Until it's time to bite.

Joseph Ash (12)
Sawston Village College

Creak

When I walk in my house,
I went upstairs because I heard a noise.
I was so scared, and very frightened,
I wondered who could be there.

I went downstairs
And then I sat down,
I picked up the phone,
So I could speak to my mum.

She said she would be back in a minute,
All I said was, 'Hurry up!'
Now I was calm,
So I turned on the light.

But then I heard the wind,
I was freaking out,
What could I do?
There was nothing here, but me all alone.

Megan Ayres (11)
Sawston Village College

Metaphor Poem

The night is . . .
Filled with shadows
Light's enemy
A mysterious atmosphere
A gloomy sky
A place where no one goes
Where spooky creatures live
A deep dark hole.

Gemma Peck (12)
Sawston Village College

Camping Holiday

Got the children to sleep at last,
I thought holidays were supposed to be a blast,
Oh no, they're up again,
'Go to sleep Millie and Ben,'
'But Mummy I need the loo,'
'Yeah,' goes Ben, 'me too,'
'Alright come on, quickly now,'
'But Mummy I stepped on a thorn, ow, ow, ow!'
'Where's your dad, is he asleep?'
'Yeah, he is, gone without a peep.'
'Oh really, alright for some,'
'Mum,' says Ben, 'I don't want to come,'
'No, I don't either,' says Millie,
'I'm fed up now,'
'Don't be so silly.'
They're back in their sleeping bags at last!
Toes all warm, feeling sleepy really fast.
'Night-night Mummy, we love you.'
'Thank you darlings, love you too.'

Claudia Cope (12)
Sawston Village College

Cricket

Come and watch some cricket
And spend some time at the wicket
Assuming of course - you have a ticket!

The batsmen are tense
Until they hit the ball to the fence

Four runs on the score
They hope for many more!

Many people play this world famous game
Wouldn't it be boring it they all played the same?

Liam Flynn (13)
Sawston Village College

Dreamcatcher

Above my head lies a delicate net
Woven with silver, silky thread
With glittering glass beads its colours are
A beautiful, shimmering little star.

All the nasty horrible dreams in my mind
Get caught inside its magical web you will find
The evil things are kept in there
It keeps me safe and in care

This gleaming net is never mean
It is and will forever be keen
To put its wonderful dreams into my head
And I can sleep in peace in my warm bed.

Luca Bogen (11)
Sawston Village College

Sweet Dreams

When I go to bed at night
I dream,
I dream of *devils* and *angels*
And places you've never seen.

When I wake up in the morning
I thank God it's Saturday,
I don't have to go to school,
I can have my own say.

Although I much prefer the dreams,
Sweet dreams,
Sweet dreams.

Alex Cracknell (13)
Sawston Village College

You Can't Be That

I told them
When I grow up
I'm not going to be a builder,
A baker or a candy stick maker
I will help birds fly
I'm going to be the sky.

I told them
When I grow up
I'm not going to be a lawyer,
A solicitor or a sumo wrestler that weighs a ton,
I'm going to be the sun.

My family does not understand me
I'll be a ghost that will give you a fright
I'll be a shadow that comes out at night
They do not realise I can fulfil any dream
I don't need to be in a team.

Amy Parker (11)
Sawston Village College

Fireworks Night

Wrapped up well in the cold night air
Hats and woollies everywhere

Then suddenly the sky is clear
A gasp, a cheer, a clap so near

Standing firmly on my feet
I feel the fireworks' inner heat

And watch them as they dance and play
Then quickly, quietly fade away.

Laura Muncey (12)
Sawston Village College

One Night

One night I was at rest,
To try and sleep my best.
Then my mum and dad said,
'I thought you hit your head.'
Then my brother came along
And yelled, 'I am really strong.'
The telephone rang,
They said it was Uncle Dan.
Then I heard the clock,
Tick-tock, tick-tock, tick-tock.
My hamster won't keep still,
He keeps running in his wheel.
My brother is so boring,
I really hate his snoring.
When my mum and dad went to sleep,
All my dad did was twitch his feet.
One night I was at rest.
To try and sleep my best.

Rachael Colbert (11)
Sawston Village College

She

She is a witch's cloak
Embroidered with silver stars
Her glistening lamp,
A moon for all below
Away she runs,
When the silence is spiked
With twitters of birds.
Who is she?
The night!

Olivia Haddow (12)
Sawston Village College

The Beach

The soft golden sand,
Gleaming in the sun,
The beach is now so calm,
It's normally busy and fun.

The sea laps on the shore,
Small waves break on the sand,
The ocean is so clear,
As if it was a pane of glass.

The sun beams down on the beach,
The sand turns white and hot,
It is too hot to walk on now,
But later it will not.

Josh Bennett (13)
Sawston Village College

The Ocean Is . . .

The ocean is a caged animal,
pouncing when she's angry,
sleeping when she's calm.

The ocean is a stunning swan,
beautiful but deadly,

The ocean is a purring cat,
happy and content with delight,

The ocean is a living person,
dancing in a summer's breeze
and whistling to a song.

Richard Simpson (13)
Sawston Village College

Can You See?

I am a maze of thoughts,
   I am a passageway to the unknown,
      I am a diary, hiding someone's secrets,
         I am the universe, a never-ending space,
            I am religion: I hold your beliefs,
               I am a monkey, always active,
                  I am a nucleus, controlling my cell,
                     I am a blank page, as I cannot be read,
                        I am everything and yet I am nothing,
                           I am inside you and everyone around.

Charlotte Arnold (11)
Sawston Village College

Night

Night is like a black blanket in the sky,
Night is like a lady walking around in a black dress.
The moon shines on the lady as she walks through the dark.
The lady walks around with her black shawl,
She throws it over her shoulder.
She finally goes home, waiting for the next night.

Amy Wright (12)
Sawston Village College

What Am I?

I blast out anything that obstructs my path,
Hitting innocent animals and plants.
I let out a roasting hot liquid that clears
The path for me to unleash hell.
I cover the surrounding country in a black,
Rough rock, which smothers everything around it.
I am a constant fire of destruction,
Raging across the land.

What am I?

Tom Hawkins (11)
Sawston Village College

You Can't Do That!

I told them,
When I grow up:
I'm not going to be an architect,
Or someone who works out lies,
No, I'm going to be way high up,
I'm going to be the sky!

They said:
You can't be that, no you can't be that!

I told them,
When I grow up:
I'm not going to be a lawyer,
Or someone who makes dishes,
No, I'm going to taste delish
I'm going to be a fish!

My friends don't understand me,
I'll be a lane if I want, running through a muddy plane,
I'll be some metal turned into a chain,
They don't realise I can fulfil any ambition.
They don't know among them
Walks a *magician!*

Tom Evans (11)
Sawston Village College

I Told Them

I told them
When I grow up
I'm not going to be a crazy Joe
Or a pilot, not even a teacher, no
Everyone will jump on me,
I'm going to be a trampoline!

I told them
When I grow up
I'm not going to be a cake baker
Or an engineer, not even a lawyer, no
Everyone's going to be scared of me,
I will toast them, burn them, I am the sire
I'm going to be fire!

I told them
When I grow up
I'm not going to be a rubbish man
Or a clown, not even a receptionist, no
Everyone will adore me,
I'm going to be the sea!

They do not understand me
I'll be an apple if I want, rotting away in the dust
Where squirting caterpillars eat their way through me
They do not believe I can fulfil my dream
They do not notice in front of them
Is a new beam.

Ross Dunsmore (11)
Sawston Village College

Fire!

Burning match left on the sofa,
A silent hiss, a viper waiting to strike.
The cushion catches alight,
A quick roar, a yawning lion.

It spreads quickly along the seat,
Flickers of light, a yellow siren.
A lampshade catches light,
A small explosion, a burst of fury.

It gets bigger,
A gang of revolutionaries
Trying to push back the police.
The chair is the next victim,
A lion trying to catch his prey
In the upstairs room.

It sneaks up the stairs ready to confront its victim,
A lion ready to pounce, waiting . . .
It slithers silently under the door,
A snake going along the sand.

The victim awakes but it's too late,
The lion pounces.
The victim is swallowed in the jaws of death,
The lion's hunger is satisfied.

Cameron Carr (12)
Sawston Village College

Rabbit

I was sitting on the wall,
Watching them all.
Then I saw one,
That had done,
The best I'd ever seen.
It wasn't mean, but it was keen,
To show off to all the rest.
When its work was done,
It said, 'That was fun,'
And hopped away somewhere,
I can't find him anywhere.
But if I do, I'll say, 'Phew,'
Then I found him.
If I was his mother I'd surely ground him,
I asked him to do another trick,
But he said, 'Which?'
So I said show me them all,
But he was not pleased,
Because he'd missed his tea.

Emma Jacobs (11)
Sawston Village College

You Can't Be That

I am a blazing stream of light,
The Devil's fork,
A zigzag of light,
On a sheet of blue background.
One strike and I can frazzle you to a crisp.
I am the cause of fear and terror everywhere.
When I arrive . . . you'll wish you never met me.

Who am I?

Lightning!

Elease Turner (12)
Sawston Village College

The Monstrous Man

Thunder and lightning,
They are his howl.
The rain is his shower,
The sun is his towel.

His shadow is darkness,
He walks in the night.
He wanders at dusk
And sleeps in the light.

No one can see him,
But feel him they can.
Sending a shiver,
The Monstrous Man!

Julia Hiom (12)
Sawston Village College

I Am . . .

I am . . .
    Fear
    Hot and raging
    A red roaring face
    A worst nightmare
    Irritation.

I am . . .
    Fury
    Rage
    Temper
    Vexation
    Annoyance.

Adam Rice (11)
Sawston Village College

The Lord Of The Storm

The clouds cracked, the thunder growled
The lightning stretched its rusty fingers
And pointed down at the Earth.

The wild westerly wind howled
And the trees sang and danced.

All of this made the animals quiver
And hide in their sheltered burrows.

The king arose, the lord of the storm
And slashed his watery weapon
Over the unexpecting houses.

His wavy body twisting this way and that
As the power swept over him.
He gave a last lash out at the world
And then retreated to his underwater lair.

The lord of the storm
Would come again.

Juliette Colaco (11)
Sawston Village College

Who Am I?

I am a black sheet,
A dark cloud over the world,
A tunnel you can't reach the end of,
I take the stars and the moon with me.

I am worst enemy with the sun,
I hate a bright, light day.
You can't feel me, only see me,
I am alive when you go to sleep,
But in the morning I am gone.

Helen Moss (11)
Sawston Village College

The Dance Of The Devil

It covers the sky with a glittering cloth,
The clouds loom over and they don't look soft.
The clouds fall dark as they black out the light,
The villagers flee in a terrible fright.

The thunder crashes as loud as a jet,
The lightning strikes, so quick you forget.
The wind blows, so hard, so strong,
The wind throws, so tiring, so long.

The Devil grins a devious smile,
The storms grow more, but just for a while.
The sun fights with the storm to stop the way,
The storm carries on and steals the day.

The sun screams as victory is near,
The storm is dead and the sky is clear.
The sun smiles as it sinks away,
The moon pops up to end the day.

The villagers drift into a deep, deep sleep,
They forget the storm, not one peep.
The moon disappears, the sun is here,
It's here to help the villagers, dear.

Kelly Lloyd (11)
Sawston Village College

Anger

Anger is a volcano getting ready to blow
Anger is a blast of rage
Anger is a tormented soul
Anger is a machine about to explode
Anger is a fiery chasm
Anger is a burst of fury
Anger is a ticking bomb . . .
    And when anger gets free, run and hide.

Ewan James Baldwin (11)
Sawston Village College

Haunted Hallowe'en

H aunted Hallowe'en
A time of fear
U nknown horrors
N ight is long and dark
T rust no one
E choes of pain
D eadly silence.

H eed the shadows
A ll seems calm
L ook further
L ook deeper
O bserve the spirit of the moment
W arnings of danger
E nter your mind
E nd your life
N ow rest.

Samantha Tovey (11)
Sawston Village College

I Am . . .

The steam pushing pistons of evil
The power that inspires terror everywhere
The driving force behind deadly creatures
The feeling that can keep you alive but also kill you
Rage, wrath and temper are my best friend
The drive to murder and slay
Death awaits anyone who stands in my path
The most powerful energy on the planet
The weapon of the damned
I work side by side with revenge
My end product is blood.
What am I?

James Postle (11)
Sawston Village College

Man With The Trolley

In the middle of the dark, gloomy night,
The trolley man wanders alone.
His trolley rattles as he walks the streets,
He mutters many things.

The scariest thing about him,
Is when he creeps to the door
And tries to open the door.
I run to the door
And lock it just in time.

He slowly gives in and walks away,
His trolley contains something.
Nobody knows what it is,
He covers it.
Whenever I see him
He is wearing the same clothes,
He scares me.

Julia Sansom (11)
Sawston Village College

My Uncle

U nlimited
N ice garden
C ool hair
L ikes swimming
E ats loads

D oesn't cook
A nita's brother
V ery kind
I nventive
D ilemma.

Karina Honey (12)
Sawston Village College

Angry Beach

The gigantic waves come crashing down,
Sending groups of stones flying.
Sky the darkest of greys
As if it were frowning.

Wind from across the ocean
Picks up the stray litter from the ground,
Throws it all along the beach,
Whipping it all around.

Swirling,
    Twirling,
        Curling,
            Hurling.

The waves are getting bigger now,
They're crashing, smashing.
The wind is getting stronger now,
It's gusty, blustery.

Freya Chaplin (14)
Sawston Village College

My Cat

Straight through the cat flap,
Under the chair,
Whizzes round the corner
And jumps in the air.
Zooms through the doorway
And sits on the settee,
To watch television
With his owner, *me!*

Alexander Scally (11)
Sawston Village College

Season Guardians

Lips as red as roses,
Skin as soft as poppy petals,
Hair a golden summer evening,
Tunic of fresh green leaves,
Smiling, radiant young as flowers,
Child of summer.
Lips as pale as apple blossoms,
Eyes as blue as forget-me-nots.
Skin a soft brown of young spring leaves,
Clothes of daffodil and poppy petals,
Old as eternity and young as time,
Spring couple.
Skin as blue as icicles,
Hair a frozen river down her back,
Clothes a carpet frost,
Eyes as icy blue daggers,
Young as the newly fallen snow,
Queen of winter.
Skin withered, gnarled and tough,
Eyes harsh like the wind.
Hair a tangled mane of leaves,
Clothes of bark and sticks,
Old as the oak trees,
Autumn old man.
These four work together,
Guarding the seasons for all eternity.

Emma Clare Pritchard (11)
Sawston Village College

The Night Of Nightmares

The clock struck midnight
Reality was no more
It gave me a terrible fright
As I woke up on the floor

Everything was shaking
As I searched inside my mind
Then I started quaking
As the truth was hard to find

As a silhouette formed
The secret came undone
Shapes were all deformed
The night of nightmares had begun

A ghostly figure was in my sight
As fear loomed upon me
It sucked away my day and light
And stole the feelings inside me

My head was spinning all around
Nothing appeared in my way
I felt my body fall to the ground
As the nightmare drifted away.

Jazmine Lightning (11)
Sawston Village College

My Hamster

D izzy my hamster, she's so cute,
I like to feed her scrummy fruit,
Z oos would definitely not suit her,
Z any, crazy fits her best,
Y ou'd better watch out because she will nest
      in your vest.

Ellie Seymour (11)
Sawston Village College

Rugby Game

Tummy churning, lacing up boots
Warm and sweaty changing rooms,
To cold and frosty air,
Looking at opposition, heart going
Beat, beat, beat.

Running out, whistle blows, game begins
Tackles low, hard, painful, in the mud
Vicious scrummage, ruck and maul
Run, quick and fast, dive, try, cheer.

Final whistle, muddy, bruised, elated
Three cheers and the shake of hands
Warm changing rooms, muddy boots
And dirty shirts
Cheers all round for the champions.

George Newnham (11)
Sawston Village College

The Headless Horseman

Riding through the sunset
Without a sneer.
The horse's feet went *clickety-clack!*
All through the year.

It all turned silent
As he rode down the street.
He went past some people
Then decided to flee
And that's the last you'll see of he.

Hannah Badcock (11)
Sawston Village College

Parrots

I don't like parrots
They're really, really rude
They're not like bunnies
Who like to eat carrots.

Although you're wearing clothes
They say you're in the nude
They always try to nip you
When you tell them off
They get their army, *parrot crew*
When you sit down
Their beady eyes stare at you
They always have a smile like a clown.

Their feathers stick out a mile
It reminds me of the river Nile
Honestly parrots are rude!

Zoe Wallis (11)
Sawston Village College

The Room

The winding stairs wind and wind into a room
It has got a big bed in it
There is a big walk-in cupboard where *it* lives
It is a big bad monster, a shadow man
So when I climb those stairs
It begins.

It bangs the windows
Flaps the curtains
It makes the railways creak
It shakes the trains
So if you climb the very long stairs
Beware of the shadow man!

Julia Harvey (11)
Sawston Village College

Dreams

I clamber into bed,
Thinking about the day before me,
Switch the light off,
Quickly shut my eyes . . .

The darkness closes around me like a sheet,
But after a minute,
A whole new world appears in my head,
Nothing I had planned . . .

Dreaming,
Just creeps upon you,
Like a fox on a hen,
I really wish it was morning . . .

Not so fast,
My head says,
We've got to carry on,
In my dream I creep up to a door . . .

I turn the handle, icy cold,
It's unlocked,
The door swings open,
Creaking . . .

I peer into the gloomy darkness
And see a little light,
I cautiously walk up to it,
Turning at every sound . . .

I touch it,
Then I tumble down, down,
Down into a tunnel,
Forever . . .

Naomi Chamberlain (11)
Sawston Village College

The Graveyard

The wind howled,
The sky was pitch-black,
A chill down my spine,
I kept looking back.

There were lots of memorials,
Made out of stone,
I felt very frightened,
I was all alone.

I saw a torch light,
Someone walked by,
I was calm and peaceful,
So I felt warm and I sighed,

The tall trees rustled,
The moon was bright,
I walked along the path,
Not a soul in sight.

I sat on the bench
And shivered with fear,
I heard footsteps from a distance,
I knew someone was near.

I started feeling sleepy,
I looked at the time,
I'd better get back,
To the pleasant home of mine.

Charlotte Robinson (11)
Sawston Village College

The Shadow

Night and day it stalks me,
A sliver of moonlight,
He's there at night,
Black out time is near.

Time to turn on the light,
He's here, he's here,
A giant in the shades of black and grey,
He's attached to me, he will not leave, he'll always stay.

Why are you circling me?
Every hour, every day,
He's my unwanted mascot,
But we are destined for each other!

At night he'll slowly shrink to nothing,
I'm happy now! But the door creaks open,
Oh no, he's back.
Seldom spoke and seldom seen,
He's searching my room looking for me.

He spots me and attaches himself,
My shadow will not leave me be.
'Why shadow are you haunting me so?'
I said as my shadow and I walked into the snow.

Patricia Rooker (11)
Sawston Village College

What Am I?

A ticking metronome
The passing of seconds
An excited dog's tail
Each number a disciple of Jesus
The dog's a working robot.

Andrew Cheung (11)
Sawston Village College

You Can't Be That

I told them
When I grow up
I'm not going to be a footballer
Or someone who lights up the dark
No people will play on me
I'm going to be a park.

I told them
When I grow up
I'm not going to be a hairdresser
Or someone who goes golfing
No, I'll swim in the sea
I'm going to be an amazing dolphin.

They do not understand me
I'll be a tree if I want to be
Or a barn if I want to be.
They do not realise I can fulfil my dream
They do not realise among them
Walks a laser beam.

Paul Golding (11)
Sawston Village College

Night Poetry

The church bells chime,
Owls twitter,
Cars zoom by on the motorway,
A firework goes off,
Church pews freezing
From the coldness of the church,
Spirits come out at the last chime of the bell,
Floorboards creak as my cat prowls around,
Ah, ah, ah, ah.

Holly Martin (12)
Sawston Village College

Happily

Happily she skipped down the street,
Happily she brought some sweets.
Happily she gave the sweets to her mum,
Happily her mum said, 'Yum.'
Happily her mum got her keys,
Happily they went out for tea.
Happily they got the bill,
Happily they paid at the till.
Happily they made their way home,
Happily they greeted their garden gnome.
Happily they went into the house,
Happily they saw a mouse.
Happily they went to bed,
Happily they didn't bump their head!

Kayleigh Owen (12)
Sawston Village College

The Night

The night crawls across the ground
on its way it makes no sound.

The owl screeches at the top of the tree
I cannot walk on my trembling feet.

A man walks into the graveyard
I stand still and hard.

He walks up to the moonlit door
and slides across the dusty floor.

He disappears
to be met with a deadly silence.

Cody Gibson (12)
Sawston Village College

Swiftly

Swiftly I ran down the street
Swiftly the cheetah ran to eat

Swiftly the star shot across the sky
Swiftly the boy ate the pie

Swiftly the hare darted across the grass
Swiftly the horses ran past

Swiftly the bouncer threw his fist
Swiftly the snake slithered and hissed

Swiftly the boy opened the book
Swiftly the mum ran and looked

Swiftly the footballer kicked the ball
Swiftly the ref said he'd broken a rule.

Ryan Stubbings (12)
Sawston Village College

My Night's Dream

I'm getting ready for bed
but what will tonight's dream bring?
Will it be good, will it be bad?
Who knows?

I'm falling asleep and . . .
I'm running to the castle.
The door opens, it's so horrible and . . .
I wake up!
Never again!

Gemma Hollidge (12)
Sawston Village College

Night

Night pounced mysteriously,
Leaping out of the darkening shadows,
Ready to annihilate his prey.
Night spoke with a whispering scream,
Hissing in an undertone to his victims,
Who he would swiftly and stealthily
Take into the world of shadows.
The shadow ghouls around him,
Looked like black hedges
Around a tree,
Swaying in a non-existent breeze.
Night then retreated,
Back to his shadow home,
Disappearing stealthily as the sun returned.

Stuart Chamley (12)
Sawston Village College

Night Is Dark

No one is out,
I can hardly see,
Ghost floating around my house.
Have you seen the black cat?
The night is one thing you cannot miss,
Is anyone awake?
Shadows nowhere,
Blank out your memories!
Listen! No sound.
A little bit of light there.
Can you see the sun?
Keep your eyes open, here comes the next day.

Rebecca Thompson (12)
Sawston Village College

The Time Stopped

I went to my room and shut the door.
The door locked.
I turned off the light and shut the window
My mind locked.

I walked and sat one side
And sat down slightly.

The time stopped, the time stopped.
There's no sound, there's no light.

Just hear the sound of breathing.
The time stopped.
My mind locked.

Boin Lee (11)
Sawston Village College

Night

Night is like a room full of dark,
the clouds are undetected,
wherever you look,
there's no one in sight.

I cannot see through
the dark, misty night,
it would help a lot,
if I could regain my sight.

The night is creeping,
like a sly, black cat,
until the day breaks through.

Mechelle Earl-Human (12)
Sawston Village College

A Teddy's Life

How I wish it was like when she was little.
We played for ages.
She was my best friend, I was hers too.
Now she's gone away to school.
I sit here alone, now she doesn't even say hello.
Sometimes she puts me on her bed.
I try to make her notice me
By trying to cuddle her when she sleeps,
But she just chucks me on the floor.
It hurts my feelings, but she doesn't know that.
I shout sometimes,
'Hello, hello.'
She can't hear me!
I'm only a stupid stuffed toy.

Hanna Taylor (13)
Sawston Village College

The Darkness

I'm afraid of the dark
I hear dogs bark
I think it's very scary
So I become really wary.

When the light is off and the door is closed
I feel the urge to dive in my covers and scream
I think a monster will come to me and will definitely start to steam.

So all in all I don't like the dark
Because right now I think I can see a shark
Argh!

James Shelford (11)
Sawston Village College

The Ocean

The ocean is like a living being,
It feels pain like a human being.
The ocean changes with each tide,
It has memories it tries to hide.

The ocean hides its secrets from the world,
It calls out to the rivers that it holds.
The ocean flows from shore to shore,
Just like you go from door to door.

The ocean can be cold and terrible,
But it can also be warm and pleasurable.
The ocean sometimes never holds back,
But subsides just like that.

The ocean is like a living being,
It spends all its time arriving and going.
The ocean changes with each tide,
It has secrets hidden beneath its depths.

Matthew Wilkinson (13)
Sawston Village College

Eyes On The Wall

Eyes on the wall stare at me,
follow me through the dark.
It's getting a bit freaky now
as I hear a greyhound bark.

I squeal, yell and run about,
I bound my way downstairs.
I fall to the ground panting, panting,
everyone crowds around me, everyone cares.

Emily Simmons (11)
Sawston Village College

Mirrored Silence

My auntie's house
the mirrored house
the ghost maiden's house.

You look in the mirror
your hair is on end
your body freezes over
as she walks past.

Many have seen her
as have I
she knows we see her
she does not like it.

As soon as you turn around
she is gone again
she will be back again
and we all know it.

She has a face of screaming silence
a face of pure anger
a face that looks wild
and bewildered that we are in her house.

Screaming as if tortured
though there is silence
all you hear is me breathing out
as she is gone again.

Adrien Webster (12)
Sawston Village College

The Victim

He sits alone thinking,
The presence of his classmates a blur to his eyes,
Only thinking one thing,
He knows they will get him.

He walks to his lessons,
Confused and fearful, not understanding,
He hasn't done anything wrong,
But he knows they will get him.

As he stares blankly,
He's wondering why, his brain is hurting,
They don't really know him,
But yet they will get him.

He'd heard the rumours,
Endured the pointing, the gossiping,
The whispers, the threats,
Everyone knows that they'll get him.

The end of the day comes,
He sees them waiting, jeering, smirking,
He tries to run, but he knows it's no good,
Now they will get him.

Lying there alone,
Crying out feebly, waiting for help,
Pain etching through his body,
He knows that they got him.

Natasha DeMartino (14)
Sawston Village College

You Can't Be That

I told them
when I grow up I'm not going to be
a firefighter or the Old Bill
I'm going to make a racket and a trill
I'm going to be a drill.

I told them
when I grow up I'm not going to be
a teacher or a preacher man
I'm going to run as fast as no one can
I'm going to be a sportsman.

I told them
when I grow up I'm not going to be
a robber or a drug dealer
I'm going to be a scrubber
or maybe even a rubber.

They do not understand me.
I'll be a tree if I want to be
or the honey from a bee.
I'll be a walk if I want to be
or the sea so people float on me.
They don't realise that in me there is a classic
they don't realise that I am magic.

Daniel Shaw (12)
Sawston Village College

Music

Music.
Like sparrows twittering high on a tree,
Swooping and sailing, as light as can be.
Twisting and turning, around and around,
Lightly and gracefully falls to the ground.

Music.
Blasting its way from the stage to an ear,
Striking and powerful, all you can hear.
Bellowing and billowing, dust falls through the room,
As the bull charges forward, bringing forth doom.

Music.
Like a wooden top turning, trilling high notes,
Spinning and twirling, like blossom it floats.
Carelessly diving, casual and free,
As the night draws in slowly, it still follows me.

Music.
Like the wind in a kite, flowing and clear,
Where is it coming from, is it far or near?
Sailing and swimming, through an all relaxed head,
It envelops the mind, clearing all that's been said.

Music.
Like a heavy sleep, it clears out the mind,
Discarding and dropping all that's not kind.
Calming and soothing, taking away pain,
The best ever medicine, again and again.

Victoria Paulding (13)
Sawston Village College

Seasons

Spring brings lambs, bleating loudly,
The pale sun shines so softly.

Summer awakens the sleepy spring air,
The sun now has a cruel, beating stare.

Autumn cools the summer's blaze,
With it brings the golden phase.

Winter encrusts the land in a snowy shell,
To the flowers we say farewell.

These are the seasons as the year goes by.
Spring is round the corner now,
Soon the rivers and lakes will flow.
God has created this, for us to enjoy,
So put on a smile, whatever the season,
There should always be happiness with every person.

Maheen Sattar (13)
Sawston Village College

Adverb Poem

Quickly, quickly, it goes very fast.
Quickly, quickly, it brakes at last.
Quickly, quickly, with all its might.
Quickly, quickly, it goes at the speed of light.
Quickly, quickly, go as fast as you can.
Quickly, quickly, catch that man.
Quickly, quickly, you've got to catch that guy.
Quickly, quickly, you've got to get that fly.
Quickly, quickly, you'd better race down that street.
Quickly, quickly, if you want to get something to eat.
Quickly, quickly, run down that road.
Quickly, quickly, get that toad.

Lee Evenden (13)
Sawston Village College

Christmas In Central Park

Snowflakes crumble from the sky,
Soon snow has iced the ground,
Like meadows weaving, lost and found.

Trees stand broad and bare,
Laced with lashings of freckled snow.

As the moon falls into night,
New York switches on its lights,
The luminous lights bedazzle the star-filled skies . . .

The polished ice, unblemished and coated with gloss,
Glows among the candyfloss snow,
As couples dance and skate in the soft moonlight.

Golden lights wrap around the Christmas tree,
Glistening in the bleak winter night.
At the tree's peak, stands a star,
Rich gold and gleaming in the darkness . . .

Chloe Pantazi (13)
Sawston Village College

Sad I Am - I Used To Be A Ford Escort

No wheel
Broken windscreen
Scratched paintwork
Door fallen off
Starter motor has been burnt out
Had a crash by going too fast and
Smashed up the back end.

Lee Graves (13)
Sawston Village College

A Winter's Night

There's a dark winter night
Inside my head,
Where the winter wolves prowl,
Taking the lives of innocent prey,
Hunting, killing, stalking!

There's a dark winter night
Inside my head,
Where no one dares to go,
Too afraid to enter the dark of night,
Darkness, freezing, night-time!

There's a dark winter night
Inside my head,
Where the icy frost bites,
Sending a chill down anyone's spine,
Quivering, shaking, chilling!

Samuel Jeffrey (13)
Sawston Village College

All Alone

Not knowing where you're going,
Stuck in a world of comings and goings,
Have no real friends, only subtitles,
No way of being like your idols,
Want to be like other people,
But they tell you to get real,
Your dreams are crushed
By the ignorance of other people,
Lip-reading's good,
But who's going to teach you?

Matt Smith (13)
Sawston Village College

The Wind

I flutter over hedges
And creep through tiny gaps,
I listen to conversations
And fly up people's backs.

I swirl like the sea,
I blow off petal blossoms,
I fly out of fans
And out of people's bottoms.

I like to rest a little,
So I stop and stare
And blow up women's skirts,
To see their underwear.

I felt nasty one day,
So I stole somebody's Kickers,
I blew up a lady's skirt,
To see she had no knickers.

I went to town for some fun,
I sent away some ants,
I blew up a Scottish kilt,
To find he had no pants.

Jonny Munden (13)
Sawston Village College

You And Me

My life is not full without you
My heart is pounding because of the love I share for you
And now that is why I've written a poem for you
You are my one and only, the only one for me
You know that we have something special
Why don't you admit it to me
So please just say *I love you.*

Daniel Chatten (11)
Sawston Village College

My Last Breath

I walk alone in the midst of night,
Just the towering street lights are in sight,
I hear footsteps creeping up behind me,
I turn around, but no, I can't see,
I carry on walking and disregard it,
But no, my judgment wasn't accurate.

I try to ignore my insanity,
But it hates me with animosity,
My breathing becomes faster now,
My defences are weaker now,
I'm running away from it all,
Now I can hear myself call.

I'm battling with myself,
I can't take much more,
I give up
And take:
My last breath.

Umit Koseoglu (13)
Sawston Village College

The Flute

The flute is long, a shiny sliver
When it is played it makes me quiver
As it is clasped in my hand
Its heavenly buttons shine bright

This is the flute that I play
The flute that says what I say
The tune's sweet, quiet, silent . . .
    Sshh
        Sshh
            Sshh
                Listen . . .

Sarah McCrae (13)
Sawston Village College

After The Rain

A blanket spread for miles,
Suffocating the sunlight,
Trapping birds and animals in its intense layers.
Azure skies and damp earth surrounding.
An emerald sea of leaves swaying together.
The distant trickle of crystal water,
Drops hitting the sodden ground,
Scurrying away.
Buzzing murmurs,
A tranquil heaven of soothing sounds.
The fresh scent of wet ground,
Undergrowth knee deep grabbing at my ankles,
Treading through intricate passages.
Lost in the peaceful hours of time,
Relaxed, dreamy and desolate.
Clammy air hangs around the canopy barrier,
Not daring to explore the world beyond.

Charley Collier (13)
Sawston Village College

Falling

She ran adrift the mist of morning,
Aloft the dewy grass and soaring.
Soaring on the silence, calling.
Calling her fear, her blight, her warning.
She found herself alight, she stumbled.
Quick and fast, a graceful tumble.
Through the air, the fog, the mist.
In the air the leaves adrift.
There she lay no more in mourning,
Still, silent, no more was she falling.
She was sleeping in unconscious danger,
Unaware, unknown to the spiteful stranger.

Rosie Ball (13)
Sawston Village College

Teenage Life

Teenage life
What a bore
'Go to your room,
Don't slam the door.'

'No way,
In a minute, maybe later'
To understand parents
You need a translator.

Why is it that
When you answer back
Your parents say
'Do you want a smack?'

'Sorry,
Dunno, can't you see?
Why do I get the blame?
It wasn't me.'

'Get out of my room'
I hold up a fist
How do I know
That I'll never be missed?

What an embarrassment
Life can be
When you're a teenager
You will see.

Daisy Ives (13)
Sawston Village College

Arranged Marriage
(Dedicated to my Maa, for reasons only some know)

When I was young my mum and dad
Sat down with me and we had a little chat.
My mother said I was promised to Miilu,
He lived with my Maa, that was all I knew.
At first, of course, I didn't understand,
But when they explained I buried my head in my hands.
My mother cried, said there was nothing she could do,
It was up to my Maa, only she could choose who.

Daddy said we were not allowed to meet till our 'day',
When the church bells would ring, and the sky would be grey.
I fought with my dad, 'I don't want to get married!'
He had no sympathy, 'It's not my problem, sorry.'
'I'm your daughter for heaven's sake! How can you watch?'
Tears streamed down my face till my skin became blotched.
But of course there was nothing he could do,
If my Maa wanted me married, then that's what I had to do.

My Maa is a very scary old lady,
With determination to do whatever she likes.
If she wants me to marry a boy called Miilu,
Then although I won't like it, that's what I'll do.
When all my friends say how my life's unfair,
I just shrug and mutter, 'No one cares.'
Which is true, I suppose, nobody does,
I'll never be someone whom a special boy loves.

Until the day I'm sixteen I'll be single, all alone,
My heart will be covered up, completely unknown.
No boy will come in, no boy will come near,
My Maa, you see, is whom they will fear.
So until the day of my dreaded fate,
My head will always be full of hate.

Katie Cheung (13)
Sawston Village College

Darkness

Night tumbles in,
Engulfing half the Earth,
Drawing forth the shadows,
Pushing out the light,
Bringing darkness.

Night flows through streets,
Across a field,
Inescapable as it moves,
Inspiring fear,
Bringing darkness.

Night walks,
A stranger in shadows,
Bringing forth demons,
Separating atoms,
Bringing darkness.

Night pounces upon the sleeping minds,
Controlling thought,
There's no return attack,
No possible surrender,
Night comes, bringing darkness.

Abigail Hunt (13)
Sawston Village College

Annoying The Teacher

Can I go to the toilet Miss?
I need to go to the toilet Miss.
Oh when can I go to the toilet Miss?
Why can't I go to the toilet Miss?
You seem to favour Jenny Miss,
Even Michael Baker Miss,
I'm bursting for the toilet Miss,
It's an emergency of importance Miss,
Even if I need to . . .
Miss, I don't need to go now!

Callum Rookes (12)
Sawston Village College

Winter Frost

She creeps and crawls like a deadly beast
Releasing her pain and anger,
Weaving through the shadow trees
Unleashing her poison breath.

Waiting many months for her turn to kill
She awaits her weakening prey,
The time has come and she spreads like fire
Liberating her frost of death.

No sound, no movement or light
The plants and creatures fall asunder,
Dreaming until the time will come
For the spring to rise again.

Lucie d'Heudieres (13)
Sawston Village College

Spirit

A drifting shadow
In the gloom.
A lonesome figure
All entombed.

An invisible cell
Holding it back,
A bewitching face
What does it lack?

A unique tale
Of a phantom, a ghost
A listless life
A shell with no host.

Jessica Smith-Lamkin (13)
Sawston Village College

A Lonely Heart

Down in the basement
In the middle of the night,
Lies a baby troll
Sleeping tight.

With bad, stinky breath
And grubby wet toes,
And gold shiny rings
Pierced in each nose.

With a lonely heart
He's waiting for whom?
As he tries to pretend
He has someone like you!

As he awakes
Cos the sun will rise,
And the spook will vanish
Before your eyes.

The next night will come
And he will appear,
Searching for someone
Far and near.

Down on the pavement
He's walking about,
And just then
He hears someone shout!

He runs along the road
Following the noise,
And there he sees
A group of boys.

There they hang
From the trunk of the tree,
While people scream
And run and flee.

There he watches
As they scream,
As he looks to the side
And sees a beam.

Then he grabs it
And hands to the boys,
And pulls them up
Still making noise.

Now they're safe
Shivering with fright,
Looking at the troll
With love and delight.

Now they're happy
Playing together,
Running and jumping
Cos they're friends forever!

Matt Teversham (11)
Sawston Village College

Alone

I lie here alone
With no one to talk to,
I sit here listening,
I hear the door open.
I'm not alone anymore,
I can talk,
Talk to someone.
I go to talk to them when, when I can't,
The only thing I can do is move.
I have no mouth, no voice,
I live alone for the rest of my life.
No one to talk to,
Laugh with or even joke with.
There's only my toys to enjoy my life with,
They're all I've got anymore,
Just my toys.

Victoria Toombs (12)
Sawston Village College

The Eagle Flies . . .

The eagle flies,
Lord of the skies.
Borne on outstretched wings,
Feathers ruffling in the wind,
He glides above the earth.

He saw the storm that 'sunk a thousand ships',
Heard a cry as it passed a baby's lips.
He smelt the smoke of a forest fire,
Felt the pain in a mourning mother's heart,
He tasted the blood of a thousand innocent souls.

He knows the sorrows that make a willow weep,
He knows the secrets that people keep.
He knows what lies beneath the ocean depths,
He knows the kings that sit on golden thrones,
He knows the beggars who are always alone.

The eagle flies,
Lord of the skies.
Borne on outstretched wings,
Feathers ruffling in the wind,
He glides above the earth.

The eagle flies . . .

Maria Reali (13)
Sawston Village College

These Huge Monsters

These huge monsters towered over me
Walked on me, jumped and lashed out on me
They were holding hands
They were grey metal giants waiting to pounce
They had four legs and six arms
They're killers waiting to strike
They attacked us with lightning - striking, striking, striking
Killing me and my father.

Josh Warner (12)
Sawston Village College

My Mates

Down the road I walk,
up the path I go,
round the corner,
up the hill
and here I am.

This Close is where my friends are from.

House number 1
is Emma's.
It's big,
not round,
tall,
not short.

House 2
is Mrs Elbes,
that evil witch she is.

House 3 is Ben's,
he's cool,
not hot.

House 4 is A's,
short for . . .
I don't know!

House 5 is Larra's,
she is randomly
strange.

House 6 is special,
it's my best mate Rachel's.

House 7 is the best though.
Why?
Because that's mine.

So now you know the Close
where all my mates live.

Tanya Browne (12)
Sawston Village College

Play With Me

I am sad
I am bad
The opposite of good
And made of wood.
No one loves me
No one cares
Full of splinters
I rot in winters.
Not knowing where to go
My only friends are garbage
No one to clean me
No one to please me.
No one to play with me
No one to stay with me
Oh, I miss the word 'playtime'.

Viktor Simonic (12)
Sawston Village College

Big Plastic Doughnut

I am a thing
That's dumped in a theme park
I have no name that I can think of
I guess I am a nut because I have no dough
I have a hole in my middle. That must be where
My heart was. I feel so sad, so lonely. If only I had
Eyes, I would cry. I'm pained to live. I wish to die. Those
Kids who jump and climb, dropping delicious doughnuts.
For I wish I had the honour, honour to be eaten. I am
Towed away because I am broken. No need, no
Need to go to hospital. I have no blood to
Spring a leak. I don't know how to end.
I am round so there is no end.
I guess I'll just have to . . .
. . .

Cameron Ford (13)
Sawston Village College

Strangely Random

Should I go this way?
Should I go that?
Should I go forward?
Should I go back?
Should I go left?
Should I go right?
I don't know,
Where should I go?

I could climb upwards,
I could dive down,
I could crawl under,
I could go asunder.
Wherever I go,
I'm back at the same place!

Lara Nugent (12)
Sawston Village College

Who Am I?

I don't know who I am, but those men in white do.
They take me everywhere, even to the loo.
I'm in an asylum, but they call it a home,
I have no freedom, the freedom to roam.
They don't know who I am and they don't know why,
Each time I talk, the words are 'goodbye'.
I hear my cellmate talking, in spite of all his might,
His will is being turned to the darkness of the night.
Till I get out of cell number 4,
Time and time again, my tears will always pour.

Yousif Oghanna (12)
Sawston Village College

Teddy Bear Tatters

I sat there quietly,
I was warm and soft,
It was all dark,
When I got dumped in the loft.

I kept hearing a strange noise,
It was a really weird sound,
It sounded like something was rattling,
Deep, deep underground.

I was left all alone,
All alone by myself,
There was no one to talk to,
But a rag doll on the shelf.

No one ever wanted me,
I was thrown under the bed,
The children played with other toys,
Like the polar bear instead.

Samantha Coupland (12)
Sawston Village College

Primary School Teachers

Aggressively giving out books!

Aggressively giving the blackboard a coat of white!
Aggressively attacking the piece of work with ticks!

Aggressively giving out marks!

Aggressively scribbling hard on the notebooks!
Aggressively asking lots of annoying questions!

Aggressively waiting for answers!

Nadiim Varsally (12)
Sawston Village College

No One Understands

No one understands when a girl is in love
With the boy of her dreams,
The one she dreamt of.
No one understands just how much she cares
About the man of her life,
But not now her friends.
No one understands that now she is happy,
She's over them all
And has left them behind.
No one understands how much she is hurting,
As her friends upped and left
And now she's alone.
No one understands how she is falling apart
With no one to talk to,
Except the one that 'she loves'.
No one understands how much she did cry
When he left her alone
And moved on his own.
No one understands what she did next,
With no one to care for,
Or no one to love.
No one understands why she did what she did,
Or how she was feeling,
As no one was there.
Well . . . maybe that's why she did it.

Kerry Chapman (15)
Sawston Village College

Save The Sea!

The sea must be strong
It lives in the wild
The sea can be rough
Or the sea can be mild.

It survives through a storm
It is cool through the heat
The sea is so strong
It is so hard to beat.

Yet we know we can beat it
With pollution and oil
The sea that's so mighty
We know how to spoil.

Some people love it
For the things they can do
Like swimming and sailing
Out in the blue.

The sea might feel lonely
Alone it must stand
But while we're asleep
It leaves tears on the sand.

We use it and need it
It's essential to live
But we don't appreciate
No thanks do we give.

So please try and help it
Escape from its fate
Do something about it
Before it's too late.

Susannah Worster (11)
Sawston Village College

Christmas

The crackers lay on the table,
all perfect and neat,
the tablecloth red,
with vegetables and meat.

The snow outside,
all fluffy and white,
the grey clouds above,
all tender and light.

The roaring fire,
all hot and warm,
cold outside,
the beginning of a storm.

Christmas Day,
my favourite of the year,
filled with presents, food
and people so dear.

Molly Wright (11)
Sawston Village College

The Table

I think I'm very useful,
Sometimes I get damaged.
I am usually kept for many years,
Sometimes something sticky is stuck to me.
I am used for holding things.
I have legs but I can't walk,
I have a flat surface,
And come in many different shapes and sizes.
Some people say that I'm boring,
But I think I'm perfect.

Kerry Bond (11)
Sawston Village College

What Am I?

What am I?
High, so high.
Can you touch me?
You'll have to fly.

See me in the day,
See me in the night.
See me in the sun,
Or in the moon's light.

What am I?
High, so high.
Can you touch me?
You'll have to fly.

My colour can change,
Black, blue or grey.
My colour can change,
Any time of day.

What am I?
High, so high.
Yes, that's right,
I am the sky.

Kayleigh Sawkins (12)
Sawston Village College

Winter's Coming Sooner Than Ever

Winter's coming sooner than ever,
Nights are getting cold,
Darkening early, no time to play,
Winter coats coming out,
People shivering but laughing too,
But Christmas is near,
Time to cheer,
Winter's coming sooner than ever!

Emily Reed (12)
Sawston Village College

What Am I?

As it creeps through the grass, the sound of its children
Echoes in the distance
Camouflaged through the silence
As it pounds upon its prey
Through the heat it sprints
To catch its children's tea

It might not be seen for those it wishes to eat
But it stands out the most of the animals
Not stripes, scales or wings for it to fly
It is the best,
As it sprints past the corner of my eye!

Rachel Chaplin (11)
Sawston Village College

The Fight

My sister and I got in a fight,
A fight to end all fights.
It began in the morning and carried on through the night,
There was a slam of the door to shake the house,
Raising our voices, we could deafen a mouse.
Dirty looks, what a sneer,
A push, a shove, I don't want her near.
The atmosphere you could cut with a knife,
Some lucky person will get her for a wife.
It is night-time now, I am feeling quite lonely,
I wish my sister were here, if only!

Thomas Andrew (11)
Sawston Village College

Always And Forever

The love for you I feel is strong
With you is where I belong
When we first talked I felt
The ground beneath me melt.
I never thought we would be
Now no one is as happy as me
Even when you do things wrong
I don't stay in a mood for long.
I want to be with you forever
And we can always be together
For eternity we can walk hand in hand
And dance upon the golden sands.
We will march right through the good and bad
And lift each other up when sad.

Hannah Griggs (15)
Sawston Village College

The Blade Of Grass

Alone is stands, a blade of grass
Among the ruthless air.
Swaying side to side.
Drops of crystal water dropped onto it
Sharp, like a knife through a heart.
Unknowing numbers walk past
Yet still unknown - anonymous
Until . . .
    Pick . . .
        Pluck . . .
            Destroyed.

Bai-Ou He (14)
Sawston Village College

Who Am I?

The rock of a chair on a bitter night,
With the purr from the cat shaking with fright,
Sharp coldness wakes me, jumping from bed,
Silent sounds getting louder I said.

A loud rhythmic sound pounding the room,
It is tense in there, please let it end soon,
Louder is the noise, the night I can't last,
Stopping, alarming slow and sometimes fast.

My frozen face and my trembling hands,
It is scaring me, please help if you can!

Have you figured out yet who I really am?

Gemma Pluck (12)
Sawston Village College

Gum

Bubble, bubble, chewing gum
Chewing, chewing bubblegum
In the town, in my bed
Chew, chew, chew, goes through my head
If everywhere on Earth I flew
I would always chew, chew

30p is all I'll need
It beats anything you could ever read
Just the sense of chew, chew, chewing
It is the best thing I could be doing
The person who gave me all this joy is Mum
So it's thanks to her for all this gum.

Nicky Savill (12)
Sawston Village College

The Armchair

I sit all day doing nothing,
Watching the goings on in the house,
Waiting for something to happen,
Waiting for the people to come home.

The house bursts into life in the evenings,
Crowding round the television,
Sitting on me,
Slopping food onto me.

I am the family's favourite chair,
I get sat on all the time,
I like the attention,
But they do hurt me sometimes.

They hurt my arms and my back,
Their huge weight sitting on top of me,
I can't move out the way,
I have to sit and take the pain.

I get worn away over time,
I start to fray and wear away,
I'm not as popular with the heavy people,
They let the cat scratch at me.

I am moved out the house and put in the car,
I am taken to a large place with lots of other old furniture,
They leave me,
I watch them drive away in the car.

I sit all day doing nothing,
But nobody ever sits on me anymore,
I am waste,
Nobody loves me.

Alistair White (14)
Sawston Village College

The Day We Went To War

On the glorious day we went to war
I'd never seen anything like it before
The sun it shone from the heavens above
The thought of war first filled me with love.

On those open plains we soldiers fought
Our country lived with one helpful thought
The bangs, the cries, the laughs, the lies,
Will be over when the final man dies.

When the last man drops down dead
The war will be over, the stories read
The noises that shook the once violent world
Will give way to peace, its white ribbon curled.

We'll hear children singing happily once more
Families will welcome their dads fondly at the door
The mothers, the brothers, the aunts and uncles too . . .
What would we men have done if we hadn't had you?

We soldiers signed up in our masses
We played our part in victorious clashes
The one thought that will forever be with me
Is of all those who worked and fought for victory.

Rebecca Blyth (14)
Soham Village College

To Hell With War!

I can't sleep
Men around me lie awake
Listening to the bellowing sounds above us
I lean against the wall of my dug-out as the earth begins to shake.

The sound of the barrage above us
Stabs through my head like a thousand knives
While guns are firing and gas shells exploding
Men sit writing last letters to their wives.

It all goes quiet
Then the whistle sounds
We carry our rifles beside us
And escape from our holes in the ground.

It's hard to see through the mist and murk
As the shells and grenades continue to drop
It's getting worse day by day
How I wish this war would stop.

Men run at us
As if it were a race
Machine guns firing
Why am I in this place?

It's time to go
So this is the end
I'm going over the top
I'll see you, my friend.

Philippa Hunter (13)
Soham Village College

Death, Pain And Silence

Do you remember . . .
The events that brought victory, loss and tears?
Do you remember . . .
The events that brought death, pain and silence?
Do you remember . . .
The dark, cold nights waiting for the signal, lying in the cold, wet, sloppy mud?
Do you remember . . .
The loud sounds which filled the emptiness of the sky, the screams, the cries?
Do you remember . . .
The cold, hard camp rations, the gooey chocolate cake, the sloppy Irish stew?
Do you remember . . .
The smell of rotting corpses from the neighbouring trenches?
Do you remember . . .
The bullets, the weapons, the cries?
Do you remember . . .
The silence of the night air, the bravery of the men who died in the frontline trenches?
Do you remember . . .
The soldiers who lost their lives fighting a war which led to death, pain and silence?
Do you remember . . .
The deadly gas attacks which also killed many men?
Do you remember . . .
The desolation of no-man's-land, that space between the frontline trenches?

I hope you'll never forget the events which led to victory, loss and tears.

I hope you'll never forget the soldiers who lost their lives fighting a war which led to death, pain and silence.

Never forget . . .

Never forget . . .

The events which led to death, pain and silence.

Alex Belshaw (13)
Soham Village College

The Poppy Fields

In the fields the poppies sway
Where glorious men gave their lives away
Let's go and knock those Germans down they would say
Then they would wave goodbye and were on their way.

Now the poppies sway as we remember them
The good, the bad, the very best of men
Up to Heaven our thanks we send
For those brave, warrior men.

We still wear poppies for those men so brave
It was us they were fighting to save
Now they lie resting in their graves
Knowing that the world is safe.

In the fields the poppies sway
Where glorious men gave their lives away
Have a look but do not play
Then say goodbye and walk away.

Hannah Rowley (13)
Soham Village College

Going Over The Top

I stumble through the never-ending sea of mud
Grenades exploding, deafening me
Shells screaming through the air above my head.
I tremble as the blast destroys our trenches
And at rifles blaring, loudly, in the air.
I hear the moaning and groaning of the injured
As wounded men lie dying all around me.
I breathe the air of war.
The trenches smell like living hell.
I salute the bravery of those soldiers
Who walk calmly on towards the enemy lines.
Others are horrified.
As they run I hear them shouting, *'We are doomed.'*
This is never going to end.

Danielle Theobald (13)
Soham Village College

Britain's Armistice

Her men will never die in vain
Will never give up hope
She will never throw away her reign
Britons will always cope.

Along the trench
The soldier goes
Through the mist and stench
While still the offensive blows.

Shells are heard
A haunting scream
Sweeps over like a bird
Then silence, a sweet dream.

Captains agree, the war is over
Britons mourn for lost comrades
Men return to London, Dover,
Britain lives again.

Hannah Sewell (14)
Soham Village College

Honour Or Pain?

Marching in the hell-driven trenches
Listening to orders we don't want to hear
Legs turned rigid with the cold and pain
What's it all for - what have we gained?

I think of the pals that I've seen die
As distant fire lights up the sky.
I've never seen Hell but I bet it's like this.

I think of the pals that I've seen die
As shells scream through the flare-lit night
I've never seen Hell but I bet it's like this.

This war is not about honour and glory
It's about land, death and pain.
What's it all for - what have we gained?

Kelly Bridge (14)
Soham Village College

The Glorious Trenches

They're really just holes in the ground
With streams of never-ending mud running through them
Where the trembling sandbags stand as walls
Separating us from the mangled barbed wire of no-man's-land.

This is what people call the trenches.

The moan of the shells coming over
Bursting dangerously near to our trench
Then the evil gas follows
A cloud of green death.

This is what people call the trenches.

The glorious posters say *'Come'*
But they have not witnessed the reality
Where you cannot stop to think.
They have not seen a friend become just another corpse
They have not heard the howling of the shells
Or felt the hammering as they hit the ground.
Here you are on a one-way ticket to Hell.

This is what people call the trenches.

Where is the glory?

Richard Clarke (13)
Soham Village College

A Taste Of The Caribbean

Hustle and bustle
In a Caribbean market
Dashing here, dashing there,
Noise and chatter
Everywhere.

Buy some fruit,
Buy some fish,
Buy some bread,
The traders said.

I closed my eyes,
Took a deep breath,
Blocked out the sounds,
And smelt.

Freshly baked bread
Freshly picked fruit
Freshly caught fish.

I found myself a mango
I felt its rough, furry skin
I put it to my mouth
And took a bite.

To my delight
It tasted
Just
Right.

Sophie Brown (12)
Soham Village College

Waiting

Every bold man starts to move.

We weave between the bodies
The gas-filled craters
The shredding barbed wire
The thunderous machine guns
We avoid the death clouds of gas.

Every bold man starts to move
To claim a few feet of land.

But we don't care
When they hit the ground, riddled with bullets
But we don't care
When they are trapped in the gas-filled craters
When they choke on the poisonous fumes that rip their lungs apart
When they are ripped apart by shrapnel
We don't care.

After all, we're only rats
Waiting.

Lewis Cotterill (13)
Soham Village College

Caribbean Riddle

Giant blue puddle floating around
Making the quietest swishing sound.
Tropical fish with flittering fins
Hoping hunting sharks won't win.
Scuttling crabs by the shore
Pinching brown fingers more and more.
Happy smiles
Shouts and cries
Overhead a seabird flies.
Giant blue puddle floating around
Making the quietest swishing sound.

Amanda King (12)
Soham Village College

It's No Show, It's War

Like a cancer fear grows bigger
Seeping its way into men's hearts and souls
Turning bravery into terror
As men prepare to cross no-man's-land.

The cold, shivering wrecks stick to their guns
As they think of what lies ahead.
No-man's-land.

Men put on brave faces
As the countdown begins
The ladders are up
Soon they will dart up out of the trench
And prance into the unknown and the unsafe
No-man's-land.

Lines of grey, muttering faces
Lined with fear
They hear the whistle to go
Into no-man's-land.

It's no show
It's war.

Sarah Claydon (14)
Soham Village College

Waiting

Three days till the shelling stops!
Three days till the attack!
I'm listening as each shell shocks another,
Men are running into no-man's-land.
It wasn't their orders, it was their mind,
They're going insane.
It's like a violent crowd and endless battle to win,
I need to get out.
Help me God!

Two days till the shelling stops!
Two days till the attack!
It's my turn on watch,
As I go to my position, a duckboard falls through.
I drop into mud, water and blood.
As I carry on, I hear the snap of a rib and then I trip.
I've trodden on the corpse of an old frontliner.
I feel like crying, knowing that he'd been gunned down,
Or hadn't had time to dine.
Help me God!

One day till the shelling stops!
One day till the attack!
Every man is tired,
With only one desire
And that is to fight!
I'm tired, but I just can't sleep,
I lie letting one eye peep.
Help me God!

Now the shelling's stopped!
It's time for the attack!
The orders are called,
'Stand to!' I put on my kit
And wait for dawn.
It's time for bombardment,
Over go the cannons and big guns,
Then come the infantry, and over I go.

We're followed by cavalry,
Charging up behind.
I hope I return!
So God, please help me . . .

Amy Ellis (14)
Soham Village College

Anancy The Trickster

Anancy the spider
Anancy the trickster
Anancy the spider
A real big fixster.

When he wants something
He'll think up a plan
He'll snatch what he needs
However he can.

Anancy the spider
Anancy the trickster
Anancy the spider
A real big fixster.

He'll double-cross you
And scuttle away
He'll always survive
To trick another day.

Ben Reed (12)
Soham Village College

Jamaican Reggae

As the beautiful fish
Swim in the sea
The steel band plays
A song for me.

It has a hip
And a hop
And a really cool beat
The rhythm is so good
I tap my feet.

The band is so loud
Others cover their ears
But me . . .
I think I'll stay here
For the rest of my years.

Arianne Martin (12)
Soham Village College

Day Ends

Square boxes
Filled with round lollipops
Hide under rectangle marshmallows
Noise of the day is shushed
By the moon.
His long arms reach for stars
Hidden in his pocket.
He scatters them all over the
Big, dark, black
Sky!

Adele Doughty (12)
Soham Village College

The Battlefield

Deep in on the battlefield
Your friends go over the top
You are then called to take their place
That's your time to drop.

Deep in on the battlefield
You find it's not a game
Shells, machine guns, snipers, rifles
Are all taking aim.

Deep in on the battlefield
Soldiers pull their triggers fast
Your friends are shot down, fall to ground
And then their time is past.

Deep in on the battlefield
Will your time be past?

Daniel Bocking (14)
Soham Village College

Why?

Is this war just a game?
Will the world ever be the same?

Why am I here?
Why does my body tremble with fear?

Why am I here?
What will happen if they bomb us?

Why am I here?
What is this never-ending curse upon us?

Why am I here?
Can't someone put a stop to this fear?

Is this war just a game?
Will the world ever be the same?

Richard Leadon (12)
Soham Village College

Sun Pride

The golden lion shakes his mane
His roaring bringing light to play.

Stars sparkle no more
The moon must say its goodbyes.
Night, like a duvet folds away.

Sunrise shines at crack of dawn,
The creatures wake from sleep,
The trees smile as the sun's rays engulf them
The sky is clear as day.

The sea is like a cat licking its paws
The sand dances around its feet
Trickling, ducking, diving.

But when the lion's gold light fades
The bear of night must come again,
To roll out the moon
And shine up the stars.

Thomas Winter (12)
Soham Village College

A Fruity Riddle

I look like a baby coconut
Although my skin is greener.

I smell as fresh as the morning
But inside me are tiny hard pips.

I feel as rough as a cat's tongue
But inside I'm full of sweet juice.

What am I?

Mary Ross (12)
Soham Village College

Your Country Needs You

We have no fear, this fight's an easy task,
In its glory we will bask.

Together we fight, we will not fail,
In the end justice will prevail.

On the map our island's small
But our empire will stand tall.

And an honour it will be
Should I die for my country.

Sacrifices must be made,
The price of freedom must be paid.

The cries of war may now be heard
But peace one day will be observed.

This beautiful country we call home
Must never again hear war's moan.

Your country needs you.

Bradley Anderson (13)
Soham Village College

Caribbean Senses

When the sun shines on the sea
The water's surface wriggles
Like a million maggots.
The taste of the fresh fruit
Makes your tongue tingle.
When you look at the sun
It burns your eyes.
The smell of the sea
Is a fresh, fishy smell.

Jamie Ingram (12)
Soham Village College

We're Off To Go To War

We're off to go to war,
To save our law,
So sign up and fight,
You know it would be right.

Give your lives for free,
For everyone and me.
Get your gun and gear,
Use without fear.

Load, aim and fire,
The enemy will tire.
Show no mercy,
Be bloodthirsty.

We advance, they retreat,
They must think they're nearly beat.
The position is clear,
Victory is near.

We've won the battle,
So never mind the prattle.
It's over Britain is proud,
Celebrate, (the streets will be loud).

Be there among the happy crowd.

Christopher Gannon (13)
Soham Village College

Men Under Fire

Men shake with fear
As they die in battle.

This is a living hell,
I wish I could be sent to Heaven.

I don't want to hear,
Roaring, howling artillery.

I don't want to feel
The ground shaking
From the crashing shells.

I don't want to hear
The men screaming with fear.

I don't want to see
Any more wounded men
Falling around me.

I wish it was over now,
I wish we had won,
I wish I was at home
With my little one.

I don't want to see
This desolate landscape,
This never-ending mud,
The shell-shocked men.

I don't want to see
The bloodstained bodies in the dark.
I hate watching my mates die.

I still think of how I served in the war,
Why my pals and not me
Had to die.

Although I am happy now,
I am having fun with my little one,
I still miss my pals.

Beccy Dobson (13)
Soham Village College

Night

Night came along
Riding a giant cat.
He jumped into the sky
And painted it black.
He looked at the sun
And knocked it
Out of the sky
With the moon.
He swept the rest of the daylight
Out of the sky
With his broom.
He dotted the sky with stars.
He jumped down to the ground
And drew everyone's curtains.
He tucked the children up in bed
And whispered goodnight.
He told them a bedtime story
About a lost kite.
By the time he had turned out
The very last light
And was finally in bed himself
It was the end
Of the night.

Matthew Taylor (13)
Soham Village College

When Our Science Teacher Left The Room!

Our science teacher left the room
And everything went mad,
Everyone was being,
So naughty and so bad!

The buzzer started buzzing,
The Bunsen started roaring,
Glass was smashing everywhere,
The wind outside was soaring!

Everything was going funny,
Things were going round the bend,
The table had just broken,
I hope that it will mend!

The bubbling of the boiling water,
The fizzing from the pot,
Everyone was screaming,
Like a baby in its cot!

Pencils started snapping,
Rulers were going *ping*,
Then *smash* goes a container
And everyone starts to sing!

The door creaked open,
Our teacher came back in,
He'd collected all the sounds we'd made,
In a very small tin!

Jess Piggott (12)
Swavesey Village College

Nothing

He liked nothing,
So did she -
Nothing.

He felt nothing,
So did she -
Nothing.

He saw nothing,
So did she -
Nothing.

He thought nothing,
So did she -
Nothing.

He was nothing,
So was she -
Nothing, nothing, nothing.

Sobia Artrey (13)
Swavesey Village College

Sadness

Clenching inside,
And feeling so small,
Wondering why,
Wanting to cry,
Remembering things,
That are now in the past,
Insides churning,
Memories turning,
Tears welling up,
Face the reality,
Not wanting her to go,
Time doesn't go slow,
Dreading this moment,
Curling so tight,
Not wanting to show,
My feelings that grow.

Olivia Jones (12)
Swavesey Village College

Let Me Think Why I Ever Loved You

I remember when I first saw you
Your face carved in my memory
My cheeks burnt a crimson hue
I wish I'd seen the other story

I remember when you first talked to me
With a mocking I didn't hear
I didn't notice you laugh at me
But now it seems so clear

I remember your first Valentine
It's words oozed with scorn
Yet I treasured every wicked line
Was I really that forlorn?

But then I opened my eyes
To see past your evil game
All those gifts had just been lies
To cut and wound and maim

Later on my birthday
You sent me a white flower
But at last I had my say
And tore it up to send you petals by the hour

And now I've got one thing to do
One last accursed itch
And that is to say to you
Get lost you ugly witch!

Peter Alston (13)
The Perse School For Boys

The Big Bang Or God?

In the beginning there was a bang,
A flash of light, a rush of rock,
Exploding across the Milky Way.

In the beginning there was darkness,
The dark was good, then God said,
'Let there be light,' and there was.

Then the molten rock made of hydrogen and helium,
Made their own gravity, pulling other rocks towards them,
Then on Earth it rained that day.

Then God separated light for the day and dark for the night,
He then said, 'Let there be oceans, rivers and streams
surrounded by land,' and there was.

That same day more rain came
And created rivers, oceans and streams,
Then some life came Earth's way.

The Earth was pleasant,
Trees and plants were planted, then God said,
'Let there be all animals of nature,' and there was.

All these tales are different views,
But combined they make the greatest of all!

Tom Wilshere (11)
The Perse School For Boys

Gen PC

Which kids are these, who do not know
Their Game Boy from their Nintendo?
Chirping birds and mountain dew
Ignored in favour of PlayStation 2.
Beethoven, Bach, Chopin and Handel
Lost, to the 500th TV channel.
Narnia, Toad of Toad Hall, and Otter -
Pushed aside by Harry Potter.
Through the earth come plants and flowers,
'But when's the next film of Austin Powers?'
Hunger, disease, paupers and lepers,
A world away from the Chilli Peppers.
Bonfire night, 'Will you light the first spark?'
'Aw, Mum, do I have to? It's South Park!'
Stories of treachery and jubilant fun
Are sidelined, until shown on BBC 1,
And likewise, tales of anguish and gore
Are only remembered via Channel 4.
'Shall we go for a drive? A swim? A ski?'
'Why? We can do it on the web for free!'
Sunday school? Lessons on Heaven?
Why listen to that, when there's S Club 7?
The world of nature is forgotten,
Replaced by EastEnders and Dot Cotton.
Bald eagle, owl, swooping vulture,
Unacknowledged by Generation Pop Culture.

Sam Baron (15)
The Perse School For Boys

Alone, But Not Home

A picture
Caught in time:
Frozen.
Forever alive,
Forever true.
No way to turn back:
He sits alone,
In the cold.
A faded checked blanket;
Wrapped tightly around his shoulders;
Snug, but still not warm.
Three day stubble,
Invades his face.
A small hat rests on his head.
A loyal dog:
Sits patiently by his side.
Never thinks of straying,
Or leaving.
Body frozen,
Everything cold.
There's no going back;
Pride stops him
All because of one argument,
A few words.
I have no father,
But he has no son.

Beatrice Bottomley (11)
The Perse School For Girls

The Spirit Of Life

The sparkling silver moon
silhouetting the high conifers
in a haze of glitter and rays
before the dawn of a golden day

On the shifting sandy plains
amid hills and twinkling stars
galloping in a stream of moonlight
rippling through the gentle night

A stallion so magnificent
with a coat of soft pine rays
rearing, floating towards the dawn
before a flame-red sun is born

A silhouette so beautiful
of the spirit of life
in a haze of glitter and rays
before the dawn of a golden day.

Helen Maimaris (12)
The Perse School For Girls

The Frost Dragon

A swirling cold mist enveloping and eating everything in its way,
you thought things were near but now they are far
you thought things with life would never die
but when the Frost Dragon comes:
Plants bow their heads and coil up in pain -
maybe next spring they'll grow again
all warmth has gone.
A chill down your spine as the Frost Dragon passes.

Do *you* know your way home?

Claire Cocks (11)
The Perse School For Girls

The School Bell

A relief
A dread
A sound

A relief for the harassed teacher
Standing, bewildered at the front of the class
'Thank goodness, now I'm rid of Robert . . .'

A dreaded sound for the class loner,
The start of 20 minutes of darkness
Courtesy of others.

It's just a sound to me
Signalling the end of a lesson,
But for others it means something.

What's the sound to you?

Harriet Lavis (12)
The Perse School For Girls

Alone

Slowly and alone
She walks the grubby pavement
Her old shoes
Hidden
By the autumn leaves
Oblivious to the world outside
She doesn't fit the scene of the busy road
Her long hair
Swaying
In the vicious wind
Her watery blue eyes
Never wander from the dirty pavement below.

Abigail Stacey
The Perse School For Girls

Autumn Fruits

The burgundy-reds
And the auburn-browns,
The large, the small
The coarse and the smooth.

Collect them in autumn
And eat them in winter,
Gone by the summer,
Growing again in spring.

Begins life in a pod,
A pea-green hedgehog,
Coiled up in a ball,
Dangling from a tree.

Plummets down
To the grass below,
Cracks open,
And out emerges
A conker.

Zosia Krasodomska-Jones (12)
The Perse School For Girls

My Hamster

My hamster is a regal hamster,
A kingly hamster,
Purchased from a palace,
Kept in a golden cage.

His name is royal,
'Herald Prospero' or 'HP'
To his lordly friends.

Delicately exercising,
On his jewelled wheel.
Stylishly sleeping
In a quilted bed.

Rosettes cover the top of his cage,
Hairy and handsome,
Best hamster in the world!

The light switch brings dark,
I crawl into bed.
I have to leave King HP sometime,
After all, he is only a hamster stuck in a golden cage.

Victoria Noble (12)
The Perse School For Girls